Engineering Software
for Accessibility

Microsoft Corporation

PUBLISHED BY
Microsoft Press
A Division of Microsoft Corporation
One Microsoft Way
Redmond, Washington 98052-6399

Copyright © 2009 by Microsoft Corporation

Library of Congress Control Number: 2009930292

A CIP catalogue record for this book is available from the British Library.

Microsoft Press books are available through booksellers and distributors worldwide. For further information about international editions, contact your local Microsoft Corporation office or contact Microsoft Press International directly at fax (425) 936-7329. Visit our Web site at www.microsoft.com/mspress. Send comments to mspinput@microsoft.com.

Microsoft, Microsoft Press, Active Accessibility, MSDN, Silverlight, Win32, Windows, Windows Server, and Windows Vista are either registered trademarks or trademarks of the Microsoft group of companies. Other product and company names mentioned herein may be the trademarks of their respective owners.

The example companies, organizations, products, domain names, e-mail addresses, logos, people, places, and events depicted herein are fictitious. No association with any real company, organization, product, domain name, e-mail address, logo, person, place, or event is intended or should be inferred.

This book expresses the author's views and opinions. The information contained in this book is provided without any express, statutory, or implied warranties. Neither the authors, Microsoft Corporation, nor its resellers, or distributors will be held liable for any damages caused or alleged to be caused either directly or indirectly by this book.

Acquisitions Editor: Ben Ryan
Developmental Editor: Devon Musgrave
Project Editor: Lynn Finnel
Editorial Production: Online Training Solutions, Inc.
Cover: Tom Draper Design

Body Part No. X15-66460

Table of Contents

What do you think of this book? We want to hear from you!

Microsoft is interested in hearing your feedback so we can continually improve our books and learning resources for you. To participate in a brief online survey, please visit:

www.microsoft.com/learning/booksurvey

What do you think of this book? We want to hear from you!

Microsoft is interested in hearing your feedback so we can continually improve our books and
learning resources for you. To participate in a brief online survey, please visit:

www.microsoft.com/learning/booksurvey

About the Authors

 Jason Grieves is a Program Manager in the Windows Accessibility Group. Jason works with students of all ages to identify their abilities rather than disabilities. In turn, he finds solutions to use those abilities to live, work, and play.

 Masahiko Kaneko is a Senior Program Manager for UI Automation. A program manager in accessibility at Microsoft for more than 10 years, he has been involved with several releases of the Windows Operating System as well as many other Microsoft products.

Technical Contributors

Larry Waldman has been a Program Manager working on Microsoft Office and accessibility for more than four years. While working on Office, he has led research in graphics accessibility, and recently became the driver for accessibility across the entire line of Office products.

Annuska Perkins is a Senior Accessibility Strategist at Microsoft. She is passionate about improving the usability and effectiveness of accessible technology solutions. She does product planning and incubation, in collaboration with business groups across Microsoft.

Greg Rolander is a programming writer in the Windows Experience division. Greg writes the documentation for the Windows SDK for the Windows Automation API, as well as several other Windows components.

Introduction

What comes to mind when you think of accessibility? If you're like most people, you might conjure up images of a wheelchair or perhaps someone who is blind. What about someone with a broken arm, a child with a learning disability, or a 65-year-old who needs high-prescription eyeglasses to read? When it comes to technology, accessibility pertains to a wide range of people with a wide range of abilities, not just the folks with disabilities.

Accessible technology is technology that users can adapt to meet their visual, hearing, dexterity, cognitive, and speech needs and interaction preferences. Accessible technology includes accessibility options and utilities built into products, as well as specialty hardware and software add-ons called assistive technology (AT) that help individuals interact with a computer.

There are essentially two types of users of accessible technology: (1) those who need it, because of disabilities or impairments, age-related conditions, or temporary conditions (such as limited mobility from a broken arm), and (2) those who use it out of preference, for a more comfortable or convenient computing experience. The majority of computer users (54 percent) are aware of some form of accessible technology, and 44 percent of computer users use some form of it, but many of them are not using AT that would benefit them (Forrester 2004).

A 2003–2004 study commissioned by Microsoft and conducted by Forrester Research found that over half—57 percent—of computer users in the United States between the ages of 18 and 64 could benefit from accessible technology. Most of these users did not identify themselves as having a disability or impaired but expressed certain task-related difficulties or impairments when using a computer. Forrester (2003) also found the following number of users with these specific difficulties:

- One in four experiences a visual difficulty.

- One in four experiences pain in the wrists or hands.

- One in five experiences hearing difficulty.

Besides permanent disabilities, the severity and type of difficulty or impairment an individual experiences can vary throughout a person's life. Table I-1 lists the four key classes of disabilities and the types of accessibility options, utilities, or AT devices your users might use to address their difficulties or impairments.

TABLE I-1   Possible AT solutions users might use to address their difficulties or impairments

Class of Disability	User Experience Without AT	Possible AT Solutions
Vision		
Mild (low vision, color blindness)	Difficulty with legibility of software and hardware interfaces	• Setting changes to font size and colors • Alternative font style and rasterization • Larger screens
Severe (blindness)	Unable to use computer monitor, need the option of receiving information through hearing or touch	• Screen reader (for text-to-speech and sound cues) • Audio description of video • Refreshable Braille display • Keyboard navigation
Dexterity		
Mild (temporary pain, reduced dexterity such as from a broken arm) to severe (paralysis, maybe carpal tunnel syndrome)	Using standard mouse or keyboard is painful or difficult	• Fine-tuning mouse and keyboard • Software (on-screen) keyboard and mouse alternative • Speech recognition utility • Alternative input device, such as a joystick or head-tracking mouse
Hearing		
Mild (hard of hearing) to severe (deaf)	Difficulty distinguishing words and sounds or not at all, need to receive information visually	• Volume adjustments • Sounds supplemented by visual cues • Multimedia captioning • Sign language
Cognitive		
Mild (learning difficulties) to severe (Alzheimer's, dementia)	Difficulty with word recognition, memory, concentration, and reasoning; UI might be overwhelming	• Reading and learning aids • Word prediction programs • Audio speech paired with visual presentation • Simplified UI • Task reminders

By 2010, the number of accessible technology users is expected to rise to 70 million, up from 57 million users in 2003 (Forrester 2004). Among users who use built-in accessibility options and utilities, 68 percent have mild or severe difficulties or impairments, whereas the remaining 32 percent have no difficulties or impairments (Forrester 2004). Among users who use AT products, such as trackballs or screen magnifiers, 65 percent did not report health issues as reasons for using AT products, but rather cited that these products make computers easier to use, more comfortable, and more convenient, or that they wish to avoid developing a future health issue (Forrester 2004).

If a majority of your users could benefit from your product being accessible, doesn't it just make sense to build an accessible product? If you have decided to do so, you are sending a message to your customers that their needs matter. Populations in many countries are getting older. Civil rights for people with disabilities are gradually being extended to encompass digital inclusion. Governments are requiring procurement officials to purchase products that are the most accessible (mandated in the U.S. by Section 508 of the Rehabilitation Act). For technology producers, creating accessible products is just the right thing to do, and it makes good business sense.

Who Should Read This Book

This book is intended to be an introduction to create accessible software products. If you want to understand how to incorporate programmatic access and keyboard access into your interfaces and how accessibility fits into the software development cycle, this book is for you. If you are a project manager or someone who is overseeing the development of an accessible product, you should also find this book helpful in understanding how accessibility is integrated at each stage of the development cycle.

What This Book Covers

As you might guess, accessibility should be integrated from the beginning of the product development cycle, when the application or product is in the planning or design phase, rather than later, when retrofitting your product for accessibility can be extremely costly—and sometimes impossible, because part of accessibility development requires attention at the architecture level. This book will guide you through the process of planning for the two critical pieces for accessibility, programmatic access and keyboard access, from the beginning of the software development lifecycle and integrating it throughout. It is, therefore, suggested that you first read the chapters in this book sequentially and then afterwards use this book as a reference as you develop your product. This book will also show you how to map out the logical hierarchy for your product and plan for implementation using UI Automation (UIA), Microsoft's accessibility API, to create products that work with assistive technologies.

Here is what to expect in each chapter:

- **Chapter 1, "The UI Automation Environment,"** provides definitions and an overview of UIA and its role in accessibility.

- **Chapter 2, "Designing the Logical Hierarchy,"** walks you through the steps for designing a logical hierarchy of your product, which will serve as a model for your accessibility implementation.

- **Chapter 3, "Designing Your Implementation,"** guides you through the process of designing the implementation of the controls in your UI.

- **Chapter 4, "Testing and Delivery,"** discusses testing for the programmatic access and keyboard access in your product and documentation for delivery, as well as a brief summary of steps for incorporating accessibility into your product.

The Basics

As mentioned, programmatic access and keyboard access are two critical pieces to accessibility and are the basis for this book. Let's go over these two areas a little further, as well as some basic information and settings you should be aware of when developing for accessibility.

Programmatic Access

Programmatic access is critical for creating accessibility in applications. Programmatic access is achieved when an application or library of UI functionality exposes the content, interactions, context, and semantics of the UI via a discoverable and publicly documented application programming interface (API). Another program can use the API to provide an augmentative, automated, or alternate user interaction. Basic information conveyed through programmatic access includes: navigation, interactive controls, asynchronous changes to the page, keyboard focus, and other important information about the UI.

Programmatic access involves ensuring all UI controls are exposed programmatically to the AT. Without it, the APIs for AT cannot interpret information correctly, leaving the user unable to use the products sufficiently or forcing the AT to use undocumented programming interfaces or techniques never intended to be used as an "accessibility" interface. When UI controls are exposed to AT, the AT is able to determine what actions and options are available to the user. Without proper programmatic access, a user may receive useless, erroneous, or even no information about what they are doing in the program.

Keyboard Access

Keyboard access pertains to the keyboard navigation and keyboard focus of an application. For users who are blind or have mobility issues, being able to navigate the UI with a keyboard is extremely important; however, only those UI controls that require user interaction to function should be given keyboard focus. Components that don't require an action, such as static images, do not need keyboard focus.

It is important to remember that unlike navigating with a mouse, keyboard navigation is linear. So, when considering keyboard navigation, think about how your user will interact with your product and what the logical navigation for a user will be. In Western cultures, people read from left to right, top to bottom. It is, therefore, common practice to follow this pattern for keyboard navigation, though there are exceptions to this practice.

When designing keyboard navigation, examine your UI, and think about these questions:

- How are the controls laid out or grouped in the UI?

- Are there a few significant groups of controls?

    o If yes, do those groups contain another level of groups?

- Among peer controls, should navigation be done by tabbing around, or via special navigation (such as arrow keys), or both?

The goal is to help the user understand how the UI is laid out and identify the controls that are actionable. If you are finding that there are too many tab stops before the user completes the navigation loop, consider grouping related controls together. Some controls that are related, such as a hybrid control, may need to be addressed at this early exploration stage. Once you begin to develop your product, it is difficult to rework the keyboard navigation, so plan carefully and plan early!

Go further: For guidelines on designing keyboard focus and keyboard navigation, go to http://go.microsoft.com/fwlink/?LinkId=150842.

Respect Your User

When developing accessible products, a key thing to keep in mind is to respect your end user's preferences and requirements. Whether they are selecting larger icons, choosing high contrast, or using a screen reader, users configure their system settings for a more comfortable user experience. It is absolutely essential, then, that you allow system-wide settings to work with your product. Overriding those settings through hard-coding might impede or even prevent a user from accessing parts of your products.

Visual UI Design Settings

When designing the visual UI, ensure that your product has a high contrast setting, uses the default system fonts and smoothing options, correctly scales to the dots per inch (dpi) screen settings, has default text with at least a 5:1 contrast ratio with the background, and has color combinations that will be easy for users with color deficiencies to differentiate.

High Contrast Setting

One of the built-in accessibility features in Microsoft's Windows operating systems is the High Contrast mode, which heightens the color contrast of text and images on the computer screen. For some people, increasing the contrast in colors reduces eyestrain and makes it easier to read. When you verify your UI in high contrast, you want to check that controls, such as links, have been coded consistently and with system colors (not with hard-coded colors) to ensure that they will be able to see all the controls on the screen that a user not using high contrast would see.

System Font Settings

To ensure readability and minimize any "unexpected" distortions to the text, make sure that your product always adheres to the default system fonts and uses the anti-aliasing and smoothing options. If your product uses custom fonts, users may face significant readability issues and distractions when they customize the presentation of their UI (through the use of a screen reader or by using different font styles to view your UI, for instance).

High DPI Resolutions

For users with vision impairments, having a scalable UI is important. UIs that do not scale correctly in high dpi resolutions may cause important UI components to overlap or hide other components and can become inaccessible. Since the release of Windows Vista, the Windows platform replaced large font settings with dpi configurations.

Go further: For more information on how to write high dpi applications, go to http://go.microsoft.com/fwlink/?LinkId=150842.

Color Contrast Ratio

The updated Section 508 of the Americans with Disability Act, as well as other legislations, requires that the default color contrasts between text and its background must be 5:1. For large texts (18-point font sizes, or 14 points and bolded) the required default contrast is 3:1.

Go further: For more information on checking color contrast, go to http://go.microsoft.com/fwlink/?LinkId=150842.

Color Combinations

About 7 percent of males (and less than 1 percent of females) have some form of color deficiency. Users with colorblindness have problems distinguishing between certain colors, so it is important that color alone is never used to convey status or meaning in an application. As for decorative images (such as icons or backgrounds), color combinations should be chosen in a manner that maximizes the perception of the image by colorblind users.

Go further: For more information on color combinations, go to http://go.microsoft.com/fwlink/?LinkId=150842.

How Accessibility Fits into the Development Cycle

Now that we've covered some of the basics, let's talk about how accessibility fits into each stage of the development cycle—requirements, design, implementation, verification, and release. You can adapt this model to the development cycle for your product. Figure I-1 provides a comprehensive view of a traditional software development cycle and activities you can do to incorporate accessibility into your product.

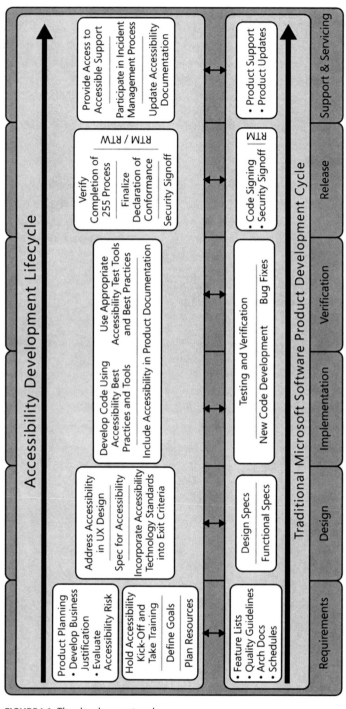

FIGURE I-1 The development cycle

Requirements Stage

There may be a variety of reasons why you may want to incorporate accessibility into your product for a variety of reasons: you want to create software that's accessible for a loved one, you hope to sell your product to the U.S. government, you want to expand your market base, your company or the law requires it, or you simply desire to do the right thing for your customers. When you decide to create a new product or update an existing one, you should know whether you will incorporate accessibility into your product.

Once you have set your requirements, generate personas that exemplify users of varying types of abilities. Create scenarios to determine what design features will delight and assist your users, and illustrate how your users will accomplish tasks with your product. Prioritize your features, and make sure that all users can complete your use cases. Beware of blanks in your specifications! Your goal is to ensure that your product will be usable by people of varying abilities.

Go further: For more information on personas, go to
http://go.microsoft.com/fwlink/?LinkId=150842.

Design Stage

In the design stage, the framework you will use is critical to the development of your product. If you have the luxury of choosing your framework, think about how much effort it will take to create your controls within the framework. What are the default or built-in accessibility properties that come with it? Which controls will you need to customize? When choosing your framework, you are essentially choosing how much of the accessibility controls you will get "for free" (that is, how much of the controls are already built-in) and how much will require additional costs because of control customizations. If accessibility was implemented in the past, look at the design docs for those earlier versions to see how accessibility features were implemented in them.

Once you have your framework, design a logical hierarchy to map out your controls (Chapter 2 covers this topic in more detail). If your design is too complex, or your framework won't even support the features that you are thinking of, it may not be worth the time, money, or effort to develop them. Accessibility can sometimes be a way to measure the usability and approachability of your product's overall design. For instance, if you are finding that the design of your keyboard navigation or logical hierarchy is becoming way too complex, it's likely that your user will have a hard time navigating your UI and will have a bad experience with your product. Go back to the drawing board, and make sure you are following fundamental user experience (UX) and accessible design practices. It's likely that somebody has already addressed the same design issues you're facing.

When you have designed your programmatic access and keyboard access implementation, ensure that all accessibility API information is noted in the specs, including all the basic development settings touched on earlier (settings for high contrast, system font defaults, a dpi-aware UI, a 5:1 text-to-background contrast ratio, and color combinations that will be easy for users with color deficiencies to differentiate). Keep in mind that it may be harder (or easier) to adhere to certain accessibility settings, depending on the framework. Programmatic access is often limited by the UI framework for the application, so it is crucial in the design stage to reconfirm the standards and expectations of the accessibility API supported by the UI framework. Keyboard navigations and the flexibility of accessibility implementations are usually tied to the architecture of the UI framework.

It is absolutely critical to note that when designing your programmatic access, *you should avoid creating new custom controls as much as possible*, because the cost for development, documentation, and help on how to interact with the control is significant, and ATs may not know how to interact with the control.

Implementation Stage

In the implementation stage, you will need to make sure that the chosen architecture and specs will work. If the specs do not work, go back to the design stage, and figure out a more effective or less expensive alternative.

When you implement the specs, be sure to keep the user experience in mind as you develop your product. Accessibility personas are great for reminding you of who your users are!

Verification Stage

In the verification or test stage, ensure that all the specs were implemented correctly and that the accessibility API is reporting correctly for programmatic access. Your accessibility API, such as UIA, must expose correctly to AT. For testing, use both accessibility test tools and full-featured, third-party accessibility aids. Write test cases and build verification tests for your accessibility scenarios to ensure that all the specs were implemented correctly.

Consider leveraging automated testing, and establish a process and metrics for accessibility bugs. You want to have clear and consistent severity ratings for these problems. Such ratings may look something like the following:

- High severity means that no workarounds are available for your target users, or the bug blocks the user from completing the task.

- Moderate severity means that workarounds are available, or that the bug does not block the user's ability to complete the operation. Do not overlook moderate severity issues, just because there is a workaround. These issues can sometimes introduce other, significant usability or product quality issues.

- Low severity means that the bug's impact to accessibility with workarounds is low.

The verification stage is a good time to start documenting all the accessibility options and features of your product. Just be sure to create documentation for your users in accessible formats! If you hope to sell your product to the U.S. government, you may also start funneling this information into a Section 508 Voluntary Product Accessibility Template (VPAT), which is a standardized form developed by the Information Technology Industry Council (ITIC) to show how a software product meets key regulations of Section 508 of the Rehabilitation Act. You absolutely want to address any high severity issues before the VPAT process, as any problems with your product will be subject to VPAT documentation.

Before your final release, be sure to obtain and incorporate feedback from your customers and partners throughout the development cycle. Include people with disabilities in your usability studies and beta testing. Work with your usability team to plan for specific accessibility studies. Include AT vendors in feedback programs, and collaborate with them to ensure that their products work with yours. Ideally, you should not need to make any major changes to your product at this stage. Any major (or expensive) changes should be reserved for your next revision.

Go further: For more information on accessibility tools and declarations of conformance, go to http://go.microsoft.com/fwlink/?LinkId=150842.

Release Stage

In the release stage, continue to engage with AT vendors and users. Include accessible documentation both internally and externally with your product, and collaborate with your marketing group on go-to-launch activities and external messaging for your product.

Ready, Set, Go!

At this point, you should now have a general understanding of what accessibility is, the types of AT your users may be relying on to use your product, the basic development settings you should include in your product, and how accessibility fits into the development cycle. You are now ready to learn more about the various components in the UIA architecture, how to design a logical hierarchy, design your implementation, and how to test your implementation and deliver your product. Through each stage of the process, you will continue to learn how to set the foundation for accessibility through programmatic access and keyboard access. For more information on the visual UI design settings mentioned earlier (such as high contrast, default font, and high dpi settings), which are also necessary for an accessible product, check out the sample of resources we provide to get you started.

Remember, designing and developing for accessibility is one of the best ways to give you clarity about the user experience in general. By creating accessible products, you are working to improve the user experience for all people. The next chapter proceeds with an introduction to UIA, Microsoft's accessibility API, which will help you integrate accessibility into your product.

Find Additional Content Online As new or updated material becomes available that complements your book, it will be posted online on the Microsoft Press Online Developer Tools Web site. The type of material you might find includes updates to book content, articles, links to companion content, errata, sample chapters, and more. This Web is available at *www.microsoft.com/learning/books/online/developer*, and is updated periodically.

Support for This Book

Every effort has been made to ensure the accuracy of this book. As corrections or changes are collected, they will be added to a Microsoft Knowledge Base article.

Microsoft Press provides support for books at the following Web site:

http://www.microsoft.com/learning/support/books/

Questions and Comments

If you have comments, questions, or ideas regarding the book, or questions that are not answered by visiting the sites above, please send them to Microsoft Press via e-mail to

mspinput@microsoft.com.

Or via postal mail to

Microsoft Press

Attn: *Engineering Software for Accessibility* Editor

One Microsoft Way

Redmond, WA 98052-6399.

Please note that Microsoft software product support is not offered through these addresses.

References

Forrester Research, Inc. 2004. "Accessible Technology in Computing: Examining Awareness, Use, and Future Potential." Cambridge, MA: 22–41.

————. 2003. "The Wide Range of Abilities and Its Impact on Technology." Cambridge, MA: 7–18.

Chapter 1
The UI Automation Environment

Intended for interoperable implementations by other companies, Microsoft's UI Automation (UIA) Community Promise is a specification that provides information about Microsoft's accessibility frameworks, including Active Accessibility (MSAA), UI Automation (UIA), and its shared implementations. In this chapter, we provide a summary of descriptions from the UIA Community Promise to show how the components of UIA fit together to enable accessibility.

UIA provides programmatic access to UI controls on the desktop, enabling assistive technology (AT) products, such as screen readers, to provide information about the UI to end users. ATs enable the user to manipulate the UI by means other than the standard mouse and keyboard, such as through speech recognition.

UIA improves upon Microsoft's legacy accessibility framework, MSAA, by aiming to address the following goals:

- Enable efficient access and security over MSAA's architecture

- Expose more robust information about the UI

- Offer interoperability with MSAA implementations

- Provide developers the option of using either native interfaces or managed interfaces

For demonstration purposes, examples are in native code (unmanaged interfaces based on COM); however, the same principles and techniques are applied to managed practices (the programming model of the Microsoft .NET Framework). Whether you will use native or managed code depends upon your framework and preferences.

Go further: For more information on the UIA Community Promise, go to http://go.microsoft.com/fwlink/?LinkId=150842.

Providers and Clients

In UIA, applications, such as word processing programs, are called *Providers*. ATs, such as screen readers, are called *Clients*. Providers expose properties and features of the UI by implementing UIA interfaces. Clients can then obtain information about the UI through a client interface from the UIA framework.

Providers communicate to Clients through UIA Events. Events are crucial for notifying Clients of changes to the UIA Tree (discussed later in this chapter), UI states, or UI controls. Unlike

WinEvents used in MSAA, UIA Events use a subscription mechanism, rather than a broadcast mechanism, to obtain information. UIA Clients register for UIA Events for specific user interfaces or even parts of the UI and can also request that some UIA Properties and Control Pattern information be cached along with registration for better performance.

Figure 1-1 is a simplified illustration of a UIA Provider and Client.

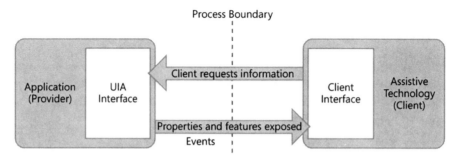

FIGURE 1-1 Simplified illustration of a UIA Provider and Client

Providers

An application may support UIA through one of two ways:

- Designing the UI based on standard framework controls and libraries that support UIA

- Implementing the UIA Provider interfaces

The following are just some of the common actions performed by UIA Providers:

- Expose UI controls by describing their functionality through Control Patterns, Properties, and Methods

- Expose the relationships of UIA Elements through the UIA Tree

- Report changes and actions related to the UI by raising UIA Events

Clients

UIA Clients can perform many different actions. The following are just some of the common actions performed:

- Search for elements within the UIA Tree

- Navigate among UIA Elements

- Subscribe to UIA Events

- Manipulate the UI by using UIA Control Patterns

Main Components

Now that you have a general sense of how UIA works, let's talk further about the main components of the framework: the Automation Elements and the UIA Tree.

Automation Elements

UIA exposes every component of the UI to Client applications as an Automation Element. Elements are contained in a tree structure, with the desktop as the root element.

Automation Elements are associated with pairs of Properties and Control Patterns, representing the functionality of an element in the UI. One of these properties is the UIA Control Type, which defines its basic appearance and functionality as a single recognizable entity, such as a button or check box. Table 1-1 lists a few Control Types and Patterns associated with a typical Automation Element.

TABLE 1-1 Example set of Control Types and Patterns associated with a typical Automation Element

Name	Control Type	Control Pattern
OK	Button	Invoke
Open	ComboBox	Value, Expand/Collapse
Installed Programs	List	Selection, Scroll

The UIA Tree

The UIA Tree allows UIA Clients to navigate through the structure of the UI. The root element of the Tree is the desktop, whose child elements are programs running on it, such as an application or the operating system's UI. Each of the child elements can contain elements representing parts of the UI, such as menus, buttons, toolbars, and lists. These elements in turn can also contain sub-elements, such as items in a list.

The UIA Tree is not a fixed structure and is seldom seen in its totality, because it might contain thousands of elements. Parts of it are built as they are needed, and it can undergo changes as elements are added, moved, or removed. UIA enables reparenting and repositioning, so that an element can move to another part of the tree, despite the hierarchy imposed by ownership of the underlying architecture.

Navigation in the UIA Tree is hierarchical: from parents to children and from one sibling to the next. UIA Providers support the UIA Tree by implementing navigation among items within a fragment, which consists of its root and sub-elements. Simple parts of the UI, however, do not need navigation implemented. The UIA framework manages navigations between fragments based on the underlying architecture.

A simple UIA Provider can be seen in Figure 1-2. Created on a Win32 framework, the Email Address window contains two child elements: the Email text label and its corresponding edit box. The Email text label and the edit box are siblings and would be positioned next to each other in the fragment of the UIA Tree. In Chapter 2, "Designing the Logical Hierarchy," we discuss in more detail why correctly mapping sibling relationships is important for navigation and giving users of AT context about the UI.

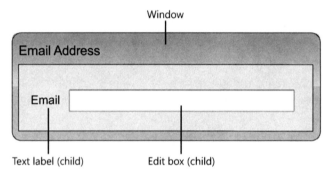

FIGURE 1-2 UIA Provider with two child elements: the Email text label and its corresponding edit box

UIA offers three default views of the UIA Tree for Clients. Clients can customize the view by defining new conditions for the UIA Properties.

- **Raw view**   The raw view is a UIA Tree with no filtering. All elements are available in this view.

- **Control view**   The control view of the UIA Tree simplifies the AT product's task of describing the UI to the end user and helping that end user interact with the application. The view maps to the UI structure perceived by an end user. It includes all Automation Elements that an end user would understand as interactive or contributing to the logical structure of the control in the UI. Examples of UI items that contribute to the logical structure of the UI, but are not interactive themselves, are list view headers, toolbars, menus, and the status bar. Non-interactive items used simply for layout or decorative purposes will not appear in the control view. An example would be a panel that is used only to lay out the controls in a dialog box, decorative graphics, and static text in a dialog box. UIA Providers can specify the elements appearing in control view by setting the UIA IsControlElement Property to True.

- **Content view**   The content view of the UIA Tree is a subset of the control view. It contains UI items that convey the true information in a UI, including UI items that can receive keyboard focus and some text that are not labels for other UI items nearby. For example, the values in a drop-down combo box will appear in the content view because they represent the information being used by an end user. UIA Providers can specify the elements appearing in content view by setting the UIA `IsContentElement` Property to True.

Control Patterns

Control patterns represent common UI behaviors (such as invoking a button) and support the properties, methods, and events. Each UIA Control Pattern is its own interface with properties and methods that provide a way to categorize and expose a control's functionality, independent of the UIA Control Type or the appearance of the control. Table 1-2 provides examples of the functionality represented by different UIA Control Patterns.

TABLE 1-2 Examples of functionality for different Control Patterns

Functionality	Control Pattern
Ability to share three states of on / off / indeterminate	`Toggle`
Ability to support a numeric value within a range	`RangeValue`
Ability to support a string value	`Value`
Ability to move / resize / rotate	`Transform`

Go further: For more information on UIA Control Patterns, go to http://go.microsoft.com/fwlink/?LinkId=150842.

Control Types

UIA Control Types are well-known identifiers that can be used to indicate what kind of control a particular element represents, such as a Button, Check Box, Combo Box, Data Grid, Document, Hyperlink, Image, ToolTip, Tree, or Window. Each Control Type has a set of conditions, which include specific guidelines for the UIA Tree, Property values, Control Patterns, and Events that a control *must* meet to use a Control Type defined in the UIA Specification.

Having a well-known identifier makes it easier for Client programs to determine what kinds of controls they must interact with in the UI. The Control Types included with UIA offer a clearer identification for the controls than ones defined by MSAA's accRole property.

Controls do *not* have to set a Control Type, however. If there is no Control Type that represents your control well, set the Control Type to "custom," and expose your control properly through the patterns and properties (including the LocalizedControlType property) that makes the most sense for your control. The UIA Specification defines required, recommended, or prohibited control patterns and properties. Custom controls can implement additional Control Patterns or Properties while being mapped to a specific Control Type.

Go further: For more information on UIA Control Types, go to http://go.microsoft.com/fwlink/?LinkId=150842.

Properties

In UIA, there are two kinds of properties that provide information about a UI element:

- **Automation Element Properties**   Properties that are applicable to most elements. For example, two properties that apply to all Automation Elements are the Name and AutomationId properties. Having these properties properly filled is highly recommended because most Clients use these properties for every Automation Element, but there may be times when the Name property may be blank for valid reasons. For example, elements used solely for layout purposes are often kept nameless, but interactive controls should not be left with a blank Name property.

- **Control Pattern Properties**   Properties specific to the functionality represented in the Control Pattern interfaces. For instance, the UIA Value Pattern will support the Value property to represent the context of controls such as a progress bar or calendar.

To ensure that you are providing the right information for clients to consume, be sure to adhere to the Specification. Certain properties have very strict requirements set. At other times, sometimes leaving the default property values is the right course of action.

Go further: For more information on UIA Properties, go to http://go.microsoft.com/fwlink/?LinkId=150842.

Events

UIA Events correspond to activities occurring in the UI and are crucial pieces of information for UIA Clients. As mentioned, UIA uses a subscription model for UIA Events; a UIA Provider will not process an Event unless a Client is listening for them. Table 1-3 lists the four different types of UIA Events.

TABLE 1-3 UIA Events

Event	Description
Property change	Raised when a UIA property changes. For example, if a Client needs to monitor an application's check box control, it can register to listen for a Property change Event on the `ToggleState` property of the Toggle Pattern. When the check box control is checked or unchecked, the property change Event for the Property gets raised.
Element action	Raised when an action is made in the UI, often related to UIA Control Patterns. For example, when an item is selected, an `ElementSelected` Event gets raised.
Structure change	Raised when the structure of the UIA Tree changes. The structure changes when new UI items become visible, hidden, or removed on the desktop.
General event	Raised when actions of global interest to the Client occur, such as when the focus shifts from one element to another, or when a window closes.

Go further: For more information on UI Automation Events, go to http://go.microsoft.com/fwlink/?LinkId=150842.

Custom Control Patterns, Properties, and Events

UIA features several Control Patterns, Properties, and Events, but the Windows implementation of UIA also offers further extensibility by registration of custom control patterns, properties, and events. As of today, this functionality is not available for managed applications of both UIA Providers and Clients.

New custom control patterns, properties, and events are only necessary if the standard UIA Control Patterns, Properties, and Events are not sufficient. Because of the extraordinary costs associated with creating new custom control patterns, properties, and events, you should avoid doing so whenever possible.

Go further: For more information on UIA Custom Control Patterns, Properties, and Events and future interoperable specifications, go to http://go.microsoft.com/fwlink/?LinkId=150842.

Planning Your Hierarchy

Now that we have covered how each of the components of UIA fit together and enable programmatic access, you are ready to learn how to design a navigational tree, called the *logical hierarchy*, for your product. In the next chapter, we walk you through the steps for designing a logical hierarchy, using an employee timecard application as an example.

Chapter 2
Designing the Logical Hierarchy

Imagine that you need to use WordPad, and you need to access it from the Start menu. How would you open the menu if you couldn't see the screen? How would you get to the application among the different items in the menu? How would you know where you were in the menu and what item your keyboard focus was on? By thinking about these questions, you have put yourself in the shoes of some of your users who need a way to navigate and interact with your UI.

Unlike users who can use a mouse and monitor to navigate the UI, users who use a screen reader primarily use a keyboard for navigating through the UI and audio devices to listen to where they are in the UI. It is, therefore, extremely important that the navigation and structure of the UI be useful, accurate, and logical. The following steps during the design phase will help to ensure that your product provides such structure and navigation:

1. Design what your UI should look like and how it will operate. The navigation and programmatic access of the UI should closely match its visual counterpart. If you make changes to the visual design, then you will need to make changes to the application's navigation and programmatic access as well.

2. Determine which UI framework you are going to use. Each framework has a different set of controls, flexibilities, and accessibility support. Depending on your UI scenarios, a particular choice may work better or worse. Take time to assess your scenarios with the framework's accessibility support. You may end up with painful costs because of your ignorance about the framework's limitations.

3. Identify the controls to create the UI. Use framework controls whenever possible and not custom controls. When using framework controls, use them as they were intended. Any irregular or nonstandard use of a control often leads to bad usability and accessibility.

4. After studying the logic of your navigation and the structure of your UI, design a *logical hierarchy*, which will enable you to plan out the accessibility in your product. An accessible solution is only possible when you fully understand the logic and structure of your own UI.

5. Plan for UI Automation (UIA) for any of your custom controls identified in step 3, including those custom controls based on framework controls. Remember that creating new custom controls is extremely costly. If you have no custom controls, you can skip this step.

In this chapter, we focus on step 4, how to design a logical hierarchy for your UI, and the next chapter walks through step 5 in detail. Both chapters may provide you with helpful information for steps 1 through 3, which may be part of the business planning and investigation of your application.

The Logical Hierarchy

What do we mean by the term "logical hierarchy?" When AT programs, such as screen readers, read your UI, visual presentation is not sufficient; you must provide a programmatic alternative that makes sense structurally to the users. A logical hierarchy can help you do that. It is a way of studying the layout of your UI and structuring each element so that users can understand it. A logical hierarchy is mainly used:

1. To provide programs context for the logical (reading) order of the elements in the UI.

2. To identify clear boundaries between custom controls and standard controls in the UI.

3. To determine how pieces of the UI interact together.

A logical hierarchy is a great way to address any potential usability issues. If you cannot structure the UI in a relatively simple manner, you may have problems with usability in your UI. A logical representation of a simple dialog box should not result in pages of diagrams. For logical hierarchies that become too deep or too wide, you may need to redesign your UI.

Figure 2-1 shows what an e-mail address window containing two child elements and its corresponding logical hierarchy looks like.

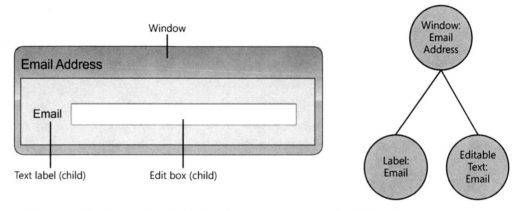

FIGURE 2-1 UIA Provider with two child elements and its corresponding logical hierarchy

When diagrammed, a logical hierarchy will look like a tree, but this "tree-like" structure should not be confused with the UIA Tree. The logical hierarchy is a tool in your specification used to help design the user experience. It is an abstraction of your application's UI and the foundation for accessible software design. Designing a logical hierarchy will also help you understand how to map the control's functionality and features in UIA, which we cover in the next chapter, and it will help to reveal any constraints or hidden costs in advance, as well.

By taking the time to identify and design the logical hierarchy of your UI, you will be on your way to turning over a very usable and accessible product.

Mapping Basics

To create a logical hierarchy, you will examine the layout of your UI to determine how you want your user to navigate through the elements. Then, for each control, you will identify whether they are common or custom controls and map them accordingly. Before we walk through these steps in greater detail, let's go over some basics you should know about elements, controls, element relationships, and navigation when mapping a logical hierarchy.

Elements and Controls

UI elements are the most basic "building blocks" in a logical hierarchy. They are either controls provided by the framework or are exposed as an element with separate functionality by other elements.

Some frameworks have controls that other frameworks do not. If you are using the framework's control as is, you do not need to break down the control any further and map out any child elements that make up that control in your logical hierarchy. The framework already provides a majority of the programmatic access for the control, so the control can be mapped as a single element. For example, because Win32 common controls have a "Menu" control, you would only need to map the Menu control as a single element.

On the other hand, in the case of a developer using HTML, the "Menu" control does not exist. So, the individual elements that make up the control, such as a menu bar, menu items, and pop-up menus, would need to be represented in a logical hierarchy to ensure that programmatic access for these items are implemented.

Naming Elements

As you learned in Chapter 1, "The UI Automation Environment," AT programs and their users depend on the Name Property of an element, so be sure to include an accessible name with each element that you map. Consistent naming practices are very important. An accessible name should be consistent with the UI text on-screen, for example.

For images and visual UI elements, the accessible name can sometimes be alternative text, which gives users context about the graphic. For instance, an icon with only an exclamation mark may have a name of "Alert" to tell users what the graphic is about.

Containers

Any element that bounds another object or group of objects is called a "container." For example, a data grid is a container, composed of individual grid items. Those individual grid items may also have elements that contain other elements.

When designing a logical hierarchy, you should only focus on containers that are useful for UI operations and providing context. Avoid including any grouping elements that are purely programmatic or only for visual design. For example, do not include a layout element that only adds redundancy or a graphical element that is hardly named (such as a background image for branding). Without these types of elements, AT clients can more easily filter elements when navigating different views of the UIA Tree.

Element Relationships and Navigation

You should already be familiar with parent/child and sibling relationships. Every element has a relationship, relative to the application window, which contains all UI elements in the application. Elements that share the same parent, such as the application window, are siblings.

The order in which sibling elements appear in the logical hierarchy is particularly important because the exact model will be used by screen readers and other AT to relay to users what they will hear and experience.

Take a look at how the elements in a data entry group box are numbered in Figure 2-2.

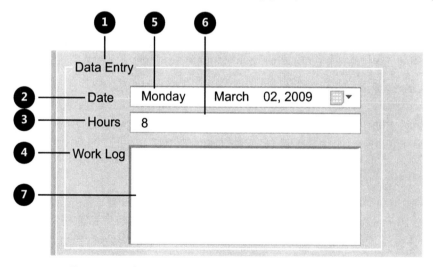

FIGURE 2-2 Elements in a data entry group box using a poor navigational order

If a screen reader were to read and follow the UI structure by the exact order in Figure 2-2, it would read the UI incorrectly, as in Figure 2-3. It may read the UI as follows: "...Data Entry, Date, Hours, Work Log, Work Log date: Monday, March 2, 2009, (blank) nameless editable text, (blank) nameless editable text..." The user would have a very difficult time trying to fill out the crucial pieces of information in their timecard. Because the Date, Hours, and Work Log labels are not read with their corresponding fields, the user may have a hard time entering information for these three things.

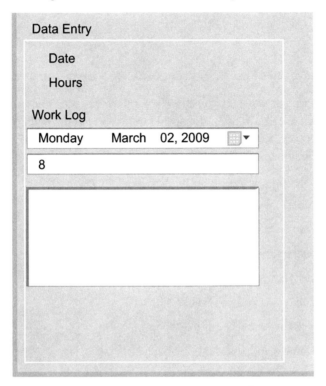

FIGURE 2-3 UI representation of a data entry group box to a screen reader following the poor navigational order of Figure 2-2

Be sure to examine the layout of your UI and the relationships between elements. How would you want your user to read through the interface? What navigational order makes the most sense? What sequence would allow a user to understand the UI most intuitively? Determine what controls relate to each other (for example, a label and its corresponding edit box). Someone who is blind must be able to navigate your UI in a logical and easy way. It is not surprising that accessible UI design shares a lot of best practices and guidelines with usability and UI design guidelines.

Standard Mapping Scheme: Top to Bottom, Left to Right

Although the standard mapping of the logical hierarchy follows a top-to-bottom, left-to-right scheme (a *depth-first search* tree traversal pattern) of the UI, AT clients can interpret the logical hierarchy however they want. That is, the clients can examine or navigate through the elements following a different pattern, such as from the bottom up or right to left. As long as the parent/child and sibling relationships are represented correctly and optimally, the logical hierarchy can be localized to fit the users' needs.

Getting Started

There are four things that you need before you start to design a logical hierarchy:

1. **Format**   How you format your logical hierarchy is up to you, but your engineering team should decide how you want it represented before you begin mapping. You can map the logical hierarchy visually using a node-link diagram (as in Figure 2-1) or textually using an outline or table format.

   Mapping in an outline format may look something like the following:

   I. Window: Product Name

   A. Element: Name (top-level child)

   B. Element: Name (top-level child)

   a. Element: Name (second-level child)

   b. Element: Name (second-level child)

   i. Element: Name (third-level child)

   C. Element: Name (top-level child)

   Mapping in a table format may look something like Table 2-1.

   TABLE 2-1 Template for Mapping in a Table Format

   Window: Product Name

Parent Element	Child Elements
Element: Name (top-level child)	Element: Name (second-level child)
	Element: Name (second-level child) • Element: Name (third-level child)
Element: Name (top-level child)	Element: Name (second-level child)

When mapping with a diagram, use the mapping symbols in Table 2-2 for your logical hierarchy.

TABLE 2-2 Logical Hierarchy Mapping Symbols

Symbol	Represents
Circle O	UI element
Solid line —	Parent/child relationship
Ellipsis ...	More siblings or repeat elements
Asterisk *	Custom control

In addition, you can use color to further differentiate custom controls from standard controls.

2. **UI prototypes**   Paper prototypes, computer drawings, UI code mockups, etc. Any prototype will do, just make sure you have enough variations of the prototype to consider different modes of the UI if there are any.

3. **Control libraries of your choice**   You will refer to the control library to determine whether a control is provided by the UI framework, as well as to help you correctly identify the control type to add to your logical hierarchy.

4. **UIA Specifications for Control Types, Patterns, and Properties**   The technical reference will help you determine whether a custom control can map to a UIA Control Type or other Properties. The specifications can be found at *http://go.microsoft.com/ fwlink/?LinkId=150842*. Table 2-3 lists 39 Control Types supported in UIA.

TABLE 2-3 Control Types supported in UI Automation

UI Automation Control Types		
Button	Image	SplitButton
Calendar	List	StatusBar
CheckBox	ListItem	Tab
ComboBox	Menu	TabItem
Custom	MenuBar	Table
DataGrid	MenuItem	Text
DataItem	Pane	Thumb
Document	ProgressBar	TitleBar
Edit	RadioButton	ToolBar
Group	ScrollBar	ToolTip
Header	Separator	Tree
HeaderItem	Slider	TreeItem
Hyperlink	Spinner	Window

How to Do It

The steps in this section should provide you with a quick start on how to design your logical hierarchy. The example that follows provides further discussion.

1. The product window is parent to all the elements contained in it. Map the product window at the top of your logical hierarchy, and label the element using its Control Type and the name you assign it, such as the "Window: Email Address" node in Figure 2-1. If you are using an outline or a table format, this element would be the first item in your outline or a header 1 (see the previous section, "Getting Started").

2. Examine the layout of your UI to determine how you want your user to navigate through the elements in it. Note which elements are grouped together or relate to one another, such as labels and their corresponding fields. Navigation between siblings should be by tab stops and arrow keys for elements within a grouping. As you design your logical hierarchy, you must ensure that the structure reflects the parent/child and sibling relationships of your UI to allow for AT users to easily navigate through it. Prototyping can help with this step.

3. Identify custom controls, whether brand new or ones that have been modified with a different functionality on an existing framework control. For instance, the Win32 list view control does not support a check box, but if you modified the control so that it does have a check box, you would identify the control as a custom control.

4. For each programmatically significant element (that is, an element necessary for UI operations or for giving ATs context), map the control type and name the element (and child elements) as follows:

   o **Standard**   Map the node as a single element if the control is based on standard control customizations. For a standard combo box, for instance, you would not need to map an element for the open and close button or list box in the control because the detailed mapping within the "combo box control" is already implied.

   o **Custom**   Map the individual elements that make up that control in the logical hierarchy, if the control is new or customized based on a standard control of the UI framework. If possible, try to find an associated UIA Control Type. Chapter 3, "Designing Your Implementation," touches more on this topic.

Table 2-4 lists a series of questions that will help you identify elements that should be included in your logical hierarchy.

TABLE 2-4 Questions to identify an element to be mapped in a logical hierarchy

Question	Considerations
Question 1: Does the framework provide the control?	If yes, map the control as a single element in your logical hierarchy, and move on to the next control in your UI. If no, proceed to Question 2.
Question 2: Does the control map to a Control Type in UIA?	Each UIA Control Type has required and optional Properties and Control Patterns. If it is difficult to map an element to a UIA Control Type, identify the types of UI functions it exhibits, and map the functionalities to the appropriate UIA Control Patterns and Properties.
	While UIA allows for a "Custom" Control Type, a control can be identified by the levels (different elements) or enhancements (different functionalities) used for the existing Control Type. For example, the RangeValue Control Pattern could be an enhancement in a combo box Control Type used to support loading status information.
	If the element does not meet any of the specifications for a UIA Control Type, consider splitting the element into sub-elements if the control is a mix of multiple Control Types, and return to Question 1 for each sub-element.
Question 3: Can you interact with parts of the control with the keyboard alone?	Every action that is provided by the mouse must also be provided by the keyboard. Be careful not to confuse selection for focus. Mouse "hot tracking" is also sometimes confused as selection or focus. If keyboard-only navigation becomes too difficult, consider an alternate way of grouping the elements in your UI or redesigning the hierarchy.
Question 4: Can the control's functionality be defined completely by Control Patterns and Properties?	You may have already answered this question in Question 2 if the element maps to a UIA Control Type. Make sure all possible Patterns and Properties are mapped based on UI scenarios and functions, and reconfirm that you're not violating rules and requirements for each Control Type specification.
	If the answer to this question is no, identify missing features and functions. Consider using a different Control Type or logical structure. Breaking down the control into smaller elements can sometimes help avoid missing features or functions.

Example: Employee Timecard

To demonstrate how to design one logical hierarchy, we will use an employee timecard application built on a Win32 framework, as an example. Figure 2-4 shows what the timecard looks like.

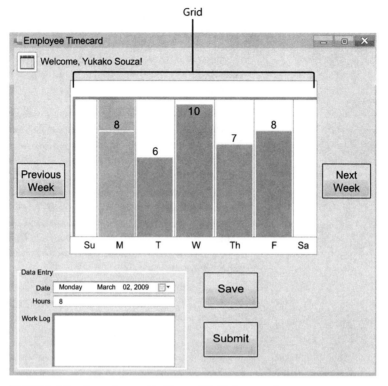

FIGURE 2-4 Employee timecard built on a Win32 framework

In the timecard, employees can:

- Click a date on the grid to see their hours or work log notes populate in the Data Entry fields.

- Use the arrow keys on the keyboard to navigate through the days in the grid.

- Enter their hours in the Hours field.

- Enter notes about their work in the Work Log field.

- Click the Previous Week button to see the previous week, and the Next Week button for the next week.

    o At the start of the fiscal year, the Previous Week button will not be available because the system archives the previous year, and employees will no longer have access to those weeks.

    o If employees are on the current week, the Next Week button will not be available because they cannot log their hours or work for future weeks.

- Save an entry without submitting.

- Submit a week for payroll review.

Except for the grid, all controls in the timecard are standard Win32 controls.

Navigational Order

Looking at the timecard, we see that there are two visual containers in the UI: the grid, made up of columns for each day of the week, and the Data Entry box, which contains the Date, Hours, and Work Log fields. Because these items are grouped together, and the fields within the container are closely related, we must ensure that the order in which we map these items must follow one another logically. Following a general top-to-bottom, left-to-right scheme, Figure 2-5 shows the navigational order in which we will map the logical hierarchy.

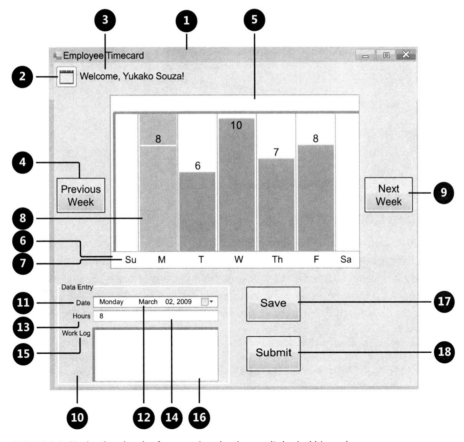

FIGURE 2-5 Navigational order for mapping the timecard's logical hierarchy

Mapping the First Element: Window

Now, we can start mapping. The window element containing the timecard application is mapped at the top of the logical hierarchy and named "Window: Timecard."

Standard Controls: First Three, Top-Level Children

The next three controls are the calendar image, the "Welcome, Yukako Souza!" label next to it, and the Previous Week push button. Looking at the Win32 control library, we see that the framework provides controls for these items, so they are standard controls and can be mapped as single elements on our logical hierarchy.

Below the window element, we plot the first three, top-level child elements from left to right according to their numerical navigational order (Figure 2-6). To indicate the parent-child relationships to the window, we draw lines from the child elements to the parent element.

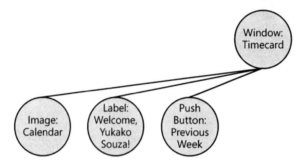

FIGURE 2-6 First three, top-level child elements of the employee timecard

Custom Control: Grid

The next control that we need to map is the grid. Looking at the Win32 control library, we see that there is not a control that captures all of the functionality of our timecard grid. It is, therefore, a custom control, which means we must break down the grid control into elements that make up the UI fragment for that control (as it might be seen in the UIA Tree). But which elements do we map? Using the questions in Table 2-4, we can identify these elements:

- Question 1: Does the framework provide the control? No. We move onto Question 2.

- Question 2: Does the control map to a Control Type in UIA? Yes. Looking at the UIA Specification for some sort of grid control, we see that our timecard grid supports the requirements for the DataGrid control. We also see that the required tree structure includes any headers and data items. In our timecard, the header is the row of labels running underneath the columns (Su, M, T, W, Th, F, and Sa), and the columns are the data items.

Our logical hierarchy now looks like Figure 2-7. Note that because there are several grid item and header elements, we mark those nodes with an ellipsis to indicate that there is more than one element for that Control Type (see Table 2-1 for mapping symbols).

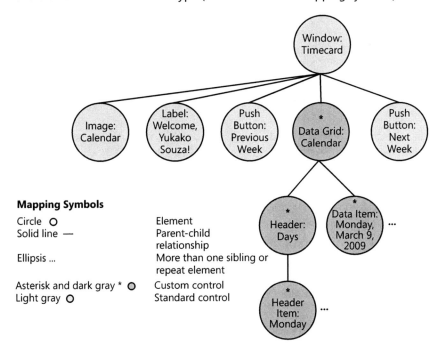

Mapping Symbols

Circle ○	Element
Solid line —	Parent-child relationship
Ellipsis ...	More than one sibling or repeat element
Asterisk and dark gray * ○	Custom control
Light gray ○	Standard control

FIGURE 2-7 Grid element added to the employee timecard's logical hierarchy

Determining the elements to map for the grid may have seemed fairly straightforward, but sometimes it is not that easy. Let's say that we weren't sure about the grid's functionality. Instead of mapping the grid to the DataGrid control, we make the mistake of identifying the columns as push buttons, because when we click them, they interact very much like push buttons. Let's see how we might have worked through this process.

- Question 1: Does the framework provide the control? No. We move onto Question 2.

- Question 2: Does the control map to a Control Type in UIA? Yes. When we click one of the columns, the interaction is very much like clicking a push button. For now, let's say that the columns are all push buttons, which can be mapped to the Button Control Type in UIA.

○   Does the element meet the UIA Control Type Specification requirements completely? No. We see that one of the Properties for the Button control is that buttons are self-labeled by their contents, as with an "OK" or "Save" button. In our timecard, our "buttons" (the clickable columns) are not labeled as such, but instead have labels with the days of the week running underneath them. We could argue that the number of hours that appear on the columns are labels for the "buttons," but the value ("8" for 8 hours, for instance) does not accurately describe the column nor is it constant (some days may not even have any hours entered, for instance). We must, therefore, start the process over again.

Taking a step back and looking at the grid as a whole, we see that that the grid is (and by definition, should be) made up of rows and columns. Each day is a clickable column, and the group of labels that runs in a row underneath the columns is actually a header for the days of the week. Looking at the UIA requirements for the DataGrid Control Type, we see that a data grid must have data items within that control. At this point, we can deduce that the clickable columns are data items (and not buttons). To verify, we check the requirements for the Control Type in the UIA Specification and confirm that the clickable columns meet the conditions for the DataItem Control Type. The columns are, in fact, data items, elements that we can map in a logical hierarchy. A close examination of the UIA Specification can save you time and answer a lot of design questions because the structures for controls are clearly defined.

Container: Data Entry Group Box

The remaining controls are all Win32 common controls and can be mapped as single, standard elements. As mentioned earlier, however, the Data Entry group box is a visual container in the UI for the Date, Hours, and Work Log fields and their corresponding labels. We must be sure to reflect these parent/child relationships in the logical hierarchy. Figure 2-8 illustrates what the completed logical hierarchy looks like for the timecard application.

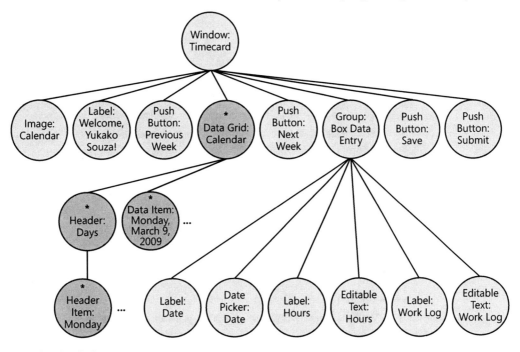

Mapping Symbols

Circle O	Element
Solid line —	Parent-child relationship
Ellipsis ...	More than one sibling or repeat element
Asterisk and dark gray * O	Custom control
Light gray O	Standard control

FIGURE 2-8 Completed logical hierarchy for employee timecard

Using the Logical Hierarchy for Planning Accessibility Settings

After plotting out the elements of your UI, the logical hierarchy can be used to assist with planning other accessibility settings, such as keyboard navigation and graphics.

Keyboard Navigation

Because your controls are already laid out in a logical hierarchy, it is easy to design your keyboard navigation. Controls that the user can interact with, such as buttons, links, or list boxes, should receive keyboard focus and may need to be part of a tab-stop loop in the keyboard navigation. Users should be able to move between controls using the TAB key and SHIFT+TAB. For grouped elements, you may need to ensure sub-navigation routines using arrow keys within two dimensional grids, or even CTRL+TAB to move between the grouped elements. If your UI supports multiple-selection, you may need to support SHIFT+RIGHT ARROW and SHIFT+LEFT ARROW key combinations.

Go further: For more information on designing keyboard navigation and UI design, go to http://go.microsoft.com/fwlink/?LinkId=150842.

Graphics: Decorative vs. Contextual

Your logical hierarchy can also help you identify decorative elements from contextual elements in your UI and the order in which they should be read by an AT program. Because the logical hierarchy is a rather primitive representation of your UI design, you should not have very many decorative UI elements in the hierarchy, because the user does not typically need to interact with graphics. Only graphics that play a crucial role in the UI's messaging should be included, such as notification or information icons, and the order of the information about the graphical information should not interfere with other important information in the UI. For instance, information about a background graphic in the UI should not appear in the logical hierarchy where it would interfere with critical information for the user. Identifying which graphics are decorative and contextual and determining where they should appear in the logical hierarchy will help with filtering any trivial elements in the object model.

Go further: UIA can filter out non-control or non-content elements by allocating elements with both the IsContentElement and IsControlElement Properties set to FALSE. For more information about how to choose and set values for those Properties, go to http://go.microsoft.com/fwlink/ ?LinkId=150842.

Complex User Interfaces

The logical hierarchy for the employee timecard that we just designed was fairly simple, but user interfaces are becoming more complex with richer functionality. As you create logical hierarchies for your UI, keep these principles in mind:

- Create logical hierarchies for all UIs that you design to ensure "seamless accessibility" for your users. Any new child window that your application creates, such as pop-up windows, should have its own logical hierarchy and accessible implementation.

- Take advantage of UI framework–provided controls and components. Just as you want to use built-in controls, using standard controls enables you to get some programmatic access "for free." Again, using these components may require you to adhere to certain accessibility guidelines and restrictions on the controls, but those have a much lower cost than a completely native UIA solution. For example, Windows Common Controls provides a list view control that can easily be implemented into your design, but the accessibility support for an irregular customization of a list view control may be extremely expensive when what you really wanted was an "engineering shortcut."

- Keep the UI as intuitive as possible. As mentioned, accessibility shares best practices and requirements with many usability and UI design guidelines. Always remember that the more complex and unique your user interface, the more work you will have to do to make it accessible. If you can accomplish your requirements in a usable, accessible, and aesthetically pleasing manner using framework controls and components, then your costs for implementation and testing will be much less than when you have to use custom controls.

Go further: For other components provided by Windows, go to http://go.microsoft.com/fwlink/?LinkId=150842.

Designing Element Functionality

Elements are the building blocks of your UI's logical hierarchy. By mapping out the programmatic access for your application in a logical hierarchy, you help to ensure that client programs, such as AT and automation tools, can navigate the UI and that users can confidently use your product. In the next chapter, we discuss how to determine the implementation of your controls, with particular focus on the design of custom controls in your logical hierarchy.

Chapter 3

Designing Your Implementation

After you have finished designing your logical hierarchy, you should know which controls in your product are provided by the UI framework and which are not. Designing the implementation of your controls depends upon this distinction:

- For controls provided by the framework, you must adhere to the UI framework's guidelines to make them accessible. For example, if you are using the Windows Presentation Foundation (WPF) framework, you would adhere to WPF's guidelines for accessibility.

- For custom controls not provided by the UI framework, you must implement a native UI Automation (UIA) solution. You have already mapped these custom controls to individual elements in the logical hierarchy, so now you must design the native UIA solution for each of these elements.

The key to designing a native solution for programmatic access is to fully expose the element's functionality so that a user of assistive technology (AT) can use the control. There are two different processes for designing the implementation of a native solution:

A. **Control maps to a UIA Control Type.**   If your custom control can map directly to a UIA Control Type, you must design the control's functionality according to the UIA Control Type Specification, including any additional requirements for other Patterns and Properties that the control may exhibit. Unless it is prohibited, a Control Type can support additional Patterns and Properties than what is required or suggested by the UIA Specification.

B. **Control does *not* map to a UIA Control Type.**   In the case where your custom control does *not* map to a UIA Control Type, then you must determine the control's functionality and design the control around the Control Patterns and Properties using the requirements of the UIA Specification. It is worth noting again that you should avoid creating new custom controls as much as possible because the cost for development, documentation, and help on how to interact with the control is significant, and ATs may not know how to interact with the control.

In this chapter, we talk about both of these design processes, focusing on controls that do map directly to a UIA Control Type. We also touch on the UIA Methods and Events that are needed to implement your controls and point you to resources for actually implementing them.

Product Example Continued: Employee Timecard

In the last chapter, we used an employee timecard, built on a Win32 framework (Figure 3-1), to design a logical hierarchy. We continue to use the timecard in this chapter to demonstrate how to design the implementation of custom controls.

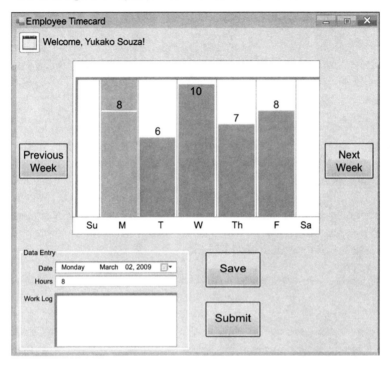

FIGURE 3-1 Product example: employee timecard built on a Win32 framework

As you may recall, all the elements in the timecard, except for the grid, were Win32 common controls. By mapping out a logical hierarchy for our timecard (Figure 3-2), we can see where custom accessibility support is needed. Because Win32 does not provide a "Grid" control, we needed to map out the individual elements that make up that the control, so that the control will expose correctly to AT.

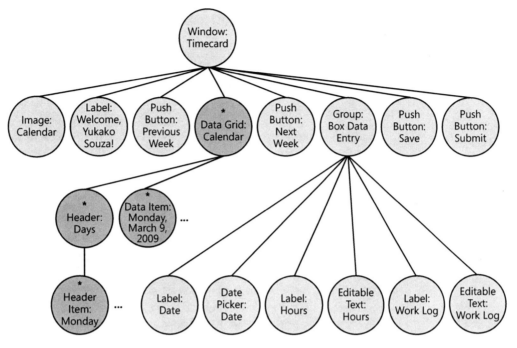

Mapping Symbols

Circle O	Element
Solid line —	Parent-child relationship
Ellipsis ...	More than one sibling or repeat element
Asterisk and dark gray * ◉	Custom control
Light gray O	Standard control

FIGURE 3-2 Logical hierarchy for the employee timecard

Prep Work: Creating the Implementation Table

By now, you should have an understanding of what Control Types, Control Patterns, and Properties are. Before we proceed, let's briefly recap these terms:

- **Control Type**   A pre-defined set of patterns, properties, and conditions used to define a control's basic appearance and functionality.

- **Control Pattern**   Defines the control's actions or behaviors.

- **Properties**   Provides specific information about the UI element or the Control Patterns supported.

When you design a native solution for a custom control in UIA, you are essentially creating an engineering "recipe" using the UIA Specification for UIA Control Types, Control Patterns,

Properties, and Events. These "ingredients" together will be used to implement an accessible custom control.

Before we proceed with designing our controls, let's do some prep work. We will create an implementation table for the primary components of the UI:

1. Create columns with the following headers:

    o   **Control**   For the elements identified as custom in your logical hierarchy.

    o   **Control Type**   For the UIA Control Type of the element.

    o   **Control Patterns**   For the required patterns necessary to implement the accessibility of the control.

    o   **Properties**   For the required automation element and control pattern properties necessary to implement the accessibility of a UI element feature.

2. Using your logical hierarchy as a reference, list each custom element in the Control column. You can omit duplicate elements, such as list items or data items that share the same characteristics with its peers. For example, the employee timecard has seven unique controls for "Grid Item: Days," but the design for each instance will be the same (except for unique Properties such as the Automation Id).

3. In the Control Type column, list the UIA Control Type that the element maps to. Again, you should have this information as a result of mapping out the logical hierarchy for your product.

Table 3-1 illustrates what the implementation table looks like for the employee timecard so far.

TABLE 3-1 Employee Timecard Custom Controls

Control	Control Type	Control Patterns	Properties	
			Automation Element Properties	Control Pattern Properties
Data Grid: Calendar	Data Grid			
Grid Item: Days	Grid Item			
Header: Days	Header			
Header Items: Days of Week	Header Item			

Process A: Control Maps to a UIA Control Type

Designing the implementation for custom controls that map to a UIA Control Type is a two-part process. You will:

1. Gather all the UIA Specification requirements for the UIA Control Type and list them in your implementation table.

2. List any additional Patterns or Properties for the controls if they exhibit any additional functionality, but make sure those additional Patterns or Properties do not contradict with the UIA Specification.

All of the controls map to UIA Control Types in our employee timecard application, so we proceed with Process A.

Step 1: Gathering Required Control Patterns

The first control in our table is the calendar grid, which maps to the DataGrid Control Type. The UIA Specification provides a table of required Patterns supported by the Data Grid Control Type (Table 3-2). We must go through each of these Patterns to verify which apply to our specific custom control.

TABLE 3-2 Required UI Automation Control Patterns for the DataGrid Control Type from the UIA Specification

Control Pattern	Support	Notes
Grid Pattern	Yes	The data grid control itself always supports the Grid Control Pattern because the items that it contains have metadata that is laid out in a grid.
Scroll Pattern	Depends	The ability to scroll the data grid depends on content and whether scroll bars are present.
Selection Pattern	Depends	The ability to select the data grid depends on content.
Table Pattern	Depends	A data grid control that has a header should support the Table Control Pattern.

Among the Patterns listed, only the Grid Pattern must always be supported by controls using the DataGrid Control Type. The Scroll Pattern, Selection Pattern, and Table Pattern, however, are dependent upon the specific data grid. Because the calendar grid in our timecard application does not scroll, the Scroll Pattern does not apply. The user can, however, select items in our grid, so the Selection Pattern also applies. Finally, our grid does support headers (which run underneath each column), so it supports the Table Pattern, as well. In our implementation table, we would, thus, list the Grid, Selection, and Table Patterns under the Control Patterns column for our timecard grid (Table 3-3).

TABLE 3-3 Required Control Patterns for the employee timecard's calendar grid custom control

Control	Control Type	Control Patterns	Properties	
			Automation Element Properties	Control Pattern Properties
Grid: Calendar	DataGrid	Grid Selection Table		

Step 2: Gathering Required Control Type Properties

The next step is to fill out our columns for the two types of Control Properties:

1. Automation Element Properties

2. Control Pattern Properties

Go further: For UI Automation Element and Control Pattern Properties, go to http://go.microsoft.com/fwlink/?LinkId=150842.

2a. Required Automation Element Properties

The Automation Element Properties listed for each Control Type is a subset of all the Automation Elements available that are likely to describe the element. The AutomationId and Name Properties appear on all Property lists for UIA Control Types. For the DataGrid Control Type, the UIA Specification lists Automation Element Properties whose value or definition is particularly relevant to DataGrid controls (Table 3-4).

TABLE 3-4 UI Automation Properties for the DataGrid Control Type from the UIA Specification

Property	Value	Notes
AutomationId	See notes	The value of this Property needs to be unique across all controls in an application.
BoundingRectangle	See notes	The outermost rectangle that contains the whole control.
ClickablePoint	See notes	Supported if there is a bounding rectangle. If not every point within the bounding rectangle is clickable, and you perform specialized hit testing, then override and provide a clickable point.
ControlType	DataGrid	This value is the same for all UI frameworks.

Property	Value	Notes
IsContentElement	True	The value of this Property must always be True. This means that the data grid control must always be in the content view of the UI Automation tree.
IsControlElement	True	The value of this Property must always be True. This means that the data grid control must always be in the control view of the UI Automation Tree.
IsKeyboardFocusable	See notes	If the control can receive keyboard focus, it must support this Property.
LabeledBy	See notes	If there is a static text label, then this Property must expose a reference to that control.
LocalizedControlType	See notes	Localized string corresponding to the DataGrid Control Type. The default value is "data grid" for en-US or English (United States).
Name	See notes	The data grid control typically gets the value for its Name Property from a static text label. If there is not a static text label, an application developer must assign a value for the Name Property. The value of the Name Property must never be the textual contents of the edit control.

For all 10 Properties, we can apply values specific to the timecard's calendar grid. For the AutomationId, BoundingRectangle, ClickablePoint, IsKeyboardFocusable, LabeledBy, Name, and LocalizableControlType Properties, which have no specified value, we must refer to the UIA Specification to find the data type for the values needed for the Property. For each of these variable Properties, we specify the Property values for the timecard in Table 3-5. Note that the ClickablePoint Property is omitted because it is irrelevant for the timecard's grid.

TABLE 3-5 Variable Automation Element Property values assigned for custom calendar grid control

Automation Element Property	Value	Data Type	Notes
AutomationId	TimecardGrid	VT_BSTR	The value for the AutomationId should be unique among siblings.
BoundingRectangle	Coordinates of table onscreen	VT_R8|VT_ARRAY	The value of the rectangle is expressed in physical screen coordinates.
IsKeyboardFocusable	False	VT_BOOL	The grid itself cannot receive keyboard focus; only the grid items can.
LabeledBy	Null	VT_UNKNOWN	Null because there is no text label for the grid.

Automation Element Property	Value	Data Type	Notes
Name	"Calendar"	VT_BSTR	Typically, the value for the **Name** Property should match the label text on screen. Because there is no on-screen label, "Calendar" is assigned. In combination with the LocalizedControlType Property, the control may read as "Calendar timecard grid."
LocalizedControlType	"timecard grid"	VT_STR	LocalizedControlType can be modified to be more understand able to the user. For English, it is suggested that the string for the LocalizedControlType Property be typed in small caps because it will be used in-line with the Name Property.

With the required Automation Element Property values now defined, you can fill out the Automation Element Properties column for the calendar grid. Table 3-6 shows what our table looks like so far.

TABLE 3-6 Implementation table with the required Automation Element Properties and their values for the employee timecard's calendar grid custom control

Control	Control Type	Control Patterns	Properties	
			Automation Element Properties	**Control Pattern Properties**
Grid: Calendar	DataGrid	Grid Selection Table	• AutomationId: TableHeader • BoundingRectangle: Coordinates of table onscreen • ControlType: DataGrid • IsContentElement: True • IsControlElement: True • IsKeyboardFocusable: False • LabeledBy: Null • LocalizedControlType: "timecard grid" • Name: "Calendar"	

Go further: For data types and properties, go to http://go.microsoft.com/fwlink/?LinkId=150842.

2b. Required Control Pattern Properties

Each Control Pattern in UIA has Properties of their own that we need to implement. Using the UIA Specification again, we can see what Properties are required for each Control Pattern and assign a value for each Pattern Property. Table 3-7 lists the Property name, value assigned, and notes about the Property for each Control Pattern.

TABLE 3-7 Control Pattern Property names and values for the timecard's calendar grid

Control Pattern	Property Name (Data Type)	Value	Notes
Grid Pattern	ColumnCount (VT_I4)	7	The total number of columns in a grid. The control has seven columns, one column for each day.
	RowCount (VT_I4)	1	The total number of rows in a grid. The control has one row of columns.
Selection Pattern	CanSelectMultiple (VT_BOOL)	False	A value that specifies whether the container allows more than one child element to be selected concurrently. The user can only select one column at a time, so the value is false.
	IsSelectionRequired (VT_BOOL)	False	A value that specifies whether the container requires at least one child item to be selected. Employees are not required to select a column when viewing their timecard, so the value is false.
Table Pattern	RowOrColumnMajor (VT_I4)	Column	The primary direction of traversal for the table. Column is chosen for the timecard because users would generally read the control by date, which is in a column.

Now that we have determined what our Property values should be for each of the calendar grid's required UIA Control Patterns, we can fill out the Control Pattern Properties column as shown in Table 3-8.

TABLE 3-8 Implementation table with the required Control Pattern Properties and their values for the employee timecard's calendar grid custom control

Control	Control Type	Control Patterns	Properties	
			Automation Element Properties	**Control Pattern Properties**
Grid: Calendar	DataGrid	Grid Selection Table	• AutomationID: TableHeader • BoundingRectangle: Coordinates of table onscreen • ControlType: DataGrid • IsContentElement: True • IsControlElement: True • IsKeyboardFocusable: False • LabeledBy: Null • LocalizedControlType: "timecard grid" • Name: Calendar	Grid Pattern • ColumnCount: 7 • RowCount: 1 Selection Pattern • CanSelectMultiple: False • IsSelectionRequired: False Table Pattern • RowOrColumnMajor: Column

Step 3: Gathering Requirements for Additional Control Functionality

Now that we have finished listing in our implementation table all the Control Patterns and Properties required by the UIA Specification for a DataGrid control, we need to list any additional Control Patterns and Properties that apply specifically to our control.

The question now is "Does my control exhibit additional functionality, aside from the required Control Patterns?" If the answer is yes, then determine what additional UIA Patterns or Properties the control maps to in UIA. If you absolutely cannot find a Control Pattern or Property that exhibits the additional functionality of your control, then you must create custom Control Patterns and Properties to describe your control, or its functionality, and include those in your implementation table. Be aware, however, that your custom specifications are only useful if UIA Clients can share and adopt your specifications. Refer to the UIA Community Promise Specification and resources from the Accessibility Interoperability Alliance (AIA) for best practices and guidance on maximizing usability.

In the case of our timecard's calendar grid, it does exhibit some additional functionality. When the user clicks one of the days in the grid, the Data Entry fields populate with any information that has been previously entered for that day. The grid affects another part of the application, the fields in the Data Entry group box. Because our grid exhibits additional functionality, we must, then, identify and map this functionality to a UIA Control Pattern or Property and list the requirements for that Pattern or Property in our implementation table. Looking at the UIA Specification, we see that the `ControllerFor` Property best describes this other functionality (Table 3-9).

TABLE 3-9 Description of the `ControllerFor` Property from the UIA Specification

Property Name (Data Type)	Description
ControllerFor (VT_UNKNOWN | VT_ARRAY)	An array of elements that are manipulated by the Automation Element that supports this Property. `ControllerFor` is used when an Automation Element affects one or more segments of the application UI or the desktop; otherwise, it is hard to associate the impact of the control operation with UI elements.

Other than the `ControllerFor` Property, our calendar grid does not appear to exhibit any additional functionality. We will go ahead and add these Properties to our table (Table 3-10).

TABLE 3-10 Completed implementation table for calendar grid custom control

Control	Control Type	Control Patterns	Properties	
			Automation Element Properties	**Control Pattern Properties**
Grid: Calendar	DataGrid	Grid Selection Table	• AutomationID: TableHeader • BoundingRectangle: Coordinates of table onscreen • ControlType: DataGrid • IsContentElement: True • IsControlElement: True • IsKeyboardFocusable: False • LabeledBy: Null • LocalizedControlType: "data grid" • **Name:** Calendar • ControllerFor: Date Picker, Hours Edit Box, and Work Log Edit Box (This Property can have multiple things.)	Grid Pattern • ColumnCount: 7 • RowCount: 1 Selection Pattern • CanSelectMultiple: False • IsSelectionRequired: False Table Pattern • RowOrColumnMajor: Column

We have now finished designing the implementation solution for our first custom control element in UIA. Before moving to the next element, it's a good idea to check the UIA Specification's list of Properties to make sure that you have listed all the requirements for your control's functionality. As mentioned, all of our custom controls in the example can map to a UIA Control Type, so we use the same process as the first control (Process A) for each of the remaining elements and fill out the rest of our implementation table (Table 3-11).

TABLE 3-11 Completed implementation table for employee timecard custom controls

Control	Control Type	Control Patterns	Properties	
			Automation Element Properties	**Control Pattern Properties**
Grid: Calendar	DataGrid	Grid Selection Table	• AutomationID: TableHeader • BoundingRectangle: Coordinates of table onscreen • ControlType: DataGrid • IsContentElement: True • IsControlElement: True • IsKeyboardFocusable: False • LabeledBy: Null • LocalizedControlType: "data grid" • Name: Calendar • ControllerFor: Date Picker, Hours Edit Box, and Work Log Edit Box (This Property can have multiple things)	Grid Pattern • ColumnCount: 7 • RowCount: 1 Selection Pattern • CanSelectMultiple: False • IsSelectionRequired: False Table Pattern • RowOrColumnMajor: Column

Control	Control Type	Control Patterns	Properties	
			Automation Element Properties	**Control Pattern Properties**
Grid Item: Days	Data Item	Grid Item Selection Item Table Item	• AutomationId: "TC#" (# is replaced by the number of the column from 1 through 7, where "TC1" would be Sunday) • BoundingRectangle: Coordinates of grid item onscreen • ClickablePoint: any point on screen clicked to select or focus the grid item reliably. • ControlType: GridItem • IsContentElement: True • IsControlElement: True • IsKeyboardFocusable: True • HasKeyboardFocus: True if the grid item is focused, false otherwise • ItemStatus: "data entered" if the grid data is entered, "empty" otherwise • LabeledBy: Null • LocalizedControlType: "timecard" • Name: date of the grid (e.g., "Mon, March 02, 2009")	Grid Item Pattern • Column: 1 through 7 • ColumnSpan: 1 • ContainingGrid: Parent Control • Row: 1 • RowSpan: 1 Selection Item Pattern • IsSelected: True if the grid item is selected, false otherwise • SelectionContainer: Parent table/grid control (No Properties for Table Item Pattern)
Header: Days	Header	None	• AutomationId: "Header" • BoundingRectangle: Coordinates of grid item onscreen • ControlType: Header • IsContentElement: False • IsControlElement: True • IsKeyboardFocusable: False • Labeled By: Null • LocalizedControlType: "header" • Orientation: Horizontal • Name: "" (Nameless because there is no other header in this control)	

Control	Control Type	Control Patterns	Properties	
			Automation Element Properties	**Control Pattern Properties**
Header Items: Days of Week	Header Item	None	• `AutomationId`: "H#" (# is replaced by the numer from 1 through 7 where H1 is for Sunday) • `BoundingRectangle`: coordinate of header item on screen • `ClickablePoint`: any point on screen clicked to select or focus the associated column • `ControlType`: HeaderItem • `IsContentElement`: False • `IsControlElement`: True • `IsKeyboardFocusable`: False • `LabeledBy`: Null • `LocalizedControlType`: "header item" • **Name**: label string of the element (e.g., "Su" for Sunday header item)	

Go further: For the UIA Community Promise and best practices and guidance on maximizing usability with interoperable implementations, go to http://go.microsoft.com/fwlink/ ?LinkId=150842.

Process B: Control Does Not Map to a UIA Control Type

So far, we have walked through designing solutions for custom controls if the controls can map directly to Control Types in UIA. What if your custom control does *not* map to a UIA Control Type? If you find yourself in this situation, then you need to take every step to be absolutely sure that your control cannot be mapped to another Control Type. To avoid unnecessary development, documentation, and help costs associated with custom controls, complete the following steps:

1. Try to identify all Patterns and Properties required to describe them.

2. Look at the UIA Control Type list again to see if there is a Control Type sufficient to map to your control. If there is a Control Type that can be used for your control, fill out the appropriate columns in your implementation table with the control's requirements.

   Note that because UIA allows you to add extra Control Patterns and Properties to an existing Control Type (unless prohibited by the UIA Control Type Specification) without making it into a completely new custom control, it is not necessary to match your custom control exactly to a UIA Control Type. You can also offer a customized description of the element based on the existing Control Type with an alternative LocalizedControlType Property value.

3. If there is absolutely no Control Type that can be used for your control, the "Custom" Control Type can be applied. Fill out the appropriate columns in your implementation table with the control's requirements, and fill out the LocalizedControlType Property with a string that would make sense to AT users.

4. Document and publish your custom Control Type specifications where it is publicly available, following the process defined by a UIA working group of the AIA, so that the specification of the custom control is clear to the users and AT makers. To facilitate the publishing process, it may also be helpful to ask a member of the AIA to publish your specification.

Methods and Events

After determining your Control Types, Patterns, and Properties, you also need to know what UIA Methods and Events are required. Methods, as you may recall from Chapter 1, provide a way to expose a control's functionality per the UIA Specification. Events in UIA are raised to notify clients, such as screen readers or screen magnifiers, that there is a change to the Automation Element in the UI. Determining these Methods and Events is straightforward and usually only requires checking the corresponding Method and Event specifications for Control Patterns and Properties that your control supports. Table 3-12 lists the Properties and Methods that are required to expose the functionality of the three Control Patterns in the timecard data grid.

TABLE 3-12 Control Properties and Methods for the employee timecard's Control Patterns

Control Pattern	Control Properties	Methods
Grid	ColumnCount RowCount	GetItem
Selection	CanSelectMultiple IsSelectionRequired	GetSelection
Table	RowOrColumnMajor	GetColumnHeaders GetRowHeaders

As you learned in Chapter 1, there are many different UIA Events. The UIA Specification directs you on what Events you must raise for your custom control. Table 3-13 lists all the Events that are supported by the data grid element and whether the Event is applicable to our timecard application.

TABLE 3-13 Data Grid UI Automation Events applicable to the timecard's custom grid control

UI Automation Event	Supported
AutomationFocusChangedEvent	Yes
BoundingRectangleProperty Property-changed Event	Yes
IsEnabledProperty Property-changed Event	Yes
IsOffscreenProperty Property-changed Event	Yes
LayoutInvalidatedEvent	Not applicable. Timecard does not invalidate the layout.
StructureChangedEvent	Yes

UI Automation Event	Supported
CurrentViewProperty Property-changed Event.	Not applicable. Timecard does not change its view mode.
HorizontallyScrollableProperty Property-changed Event	Not applicable. Timecard does not support scrolling.
HorizontalScrollPercentProperty Property-changed Event	Not applicable. Timecard does not support scrolling.
HorizontalViewSizeProperty Property-changed Event	Not applicable. Timecard does not support scrolling.
VerticalScrollPercentProperty Property-changed Event	Not applicable. Timecard does not support scrolling.
VerticallyScrollableProperty Property-changed Event	Not applicable. Timecard does not support scrolling.
VerticalViewSizeProperty Property-changed Event	Not applicable. Timecard does not support scrolling.
InvalidatedEvent	Yes

Framework-Dependent Decisions

This chapter focused on designing your custom controls to meet the UIA Specification, but the design stage does not stop here. Three areas that are framework-dependent that must be determined (if they have not already been determined) are:

1. Your framework's requirements for providing programmatic access to the controls, whether provided by the framework or custom. While standard controls of the UI framework may support the basics for programmatic access, the flexibility for accessibility can be limited to modifications.

2. Determine how UI elements will handle keyboard focus. Controls that are actionable, such as buttons and links, should receive keyboard focus. For Win32 common controls, use the control styles in the resource file, and handle the system focus as needed.

3. Ensure that your UI adheres to other accessibility requirements discussed in the introduction of this book, such as high contrast, high dpi, and other system settings.

Once you have addressed these three areas, you are ready to take your designs into the implementation stage.

Go further: For more information on adhering to accessibility requirements other than programmatic access, go to http://go.microsoft.com/fwlink/?LinkId=150842.

Implementing Your Native UIA Solution

Your next challenge is determining how to implement the native solutions you have designed over the last two chapters. How does your design actually map out to its implementation? How do you take the requirements in your implementation table and actually use the UIA framework to implement it? Because implementation is framework-dependent, this book does not provide specific implementation details, but depending on the complexity of your control, you do need to implement one or more of the UIA interfaces. These interfaces allow you to implement the Control Patterns, Properties, Methods, and Events that you specified in your implementation table.

Go further: For more information on how to implement your solution, go to http://go.microsoft.com/fwlink/?LinkId=150842.

Rounding Up Native Solutions

As you design a logical hierarchy, you can see which controls are provided by the UI framework and which are not. For controls that are not provided by the framework, you must create a native accessibility solution to implement those controls. In this chapter, we walked through the process of designing your implementation for those controls in UIA:

- For custom controls that map to a UIA Control Type, refer to the UI Automation Specifications and list all the Patterns and Properties necessary. If your control exhibits additional functionality other than those required by the UIA Specifications, then you must also include those Patterns and Properties in your table.

- For custom controls that do not map to a UIA Control Type, you must identify and map the functionality to Control Patterns or Properties that best exhibits the functionality of your custom control and list those requirements in your implementation table.

Methods and Events are required for completing your UIA implementation. Although you still need to specify how you will implement Methods and Events, the UIA Specifications detail which Methods and Events are required for the specific Control Patterns and Properties.

Implementation for each custom control varies, so after designing the native solutions for your custom controls, refer to the MSDN Web site on how to take your custom controls from the design stage to actually implementing them in your product. The next chapter provides a more in-depth discussion about testing the programmatic access and keyboard access of your implementation and delivery of your product.

Go further: For common frameworks and their accessibility guidelines, go to http://go.microsoft.com/fwlink/?LinkId=150842.

Chapter 4
Testing and Delivery

In our final chapter, we end with a discussion on testing the programmatic access of the UI and the keyboard access in your product. Testing for these two things can be done through a combination of software test tools, manual testing, and user scenario testing with assistive technology (AT) devices. In addition, we discuss documenting your implementation for delivery and summarize our recommendation for incorporating accessibility into your product in seven steps.

When it comes time to test your product, you want to focus on the most critical requirements or scenarios for your product first. For software that is complex, focus on the parts that are most critical to your scenarios or are most commonly used (for example, the Start menu in Windows). Once your core scenarios have been tested and verified, you can move onto any secondary requirements or scenarios.

Programmatic access and keyboard access are two critical requirements for accessibility. Without them, many different users of AT (such as screen reader and on-screen keyboard users) would be affected and would not be able to use your product at all.

To test programmatic access that is designed using UI Automation (UIA) on a Windows platform, Microsoft offers two types of test tools: (1) investigation tools and (2) a UIA testing framework called UIA Verify. Investigation tools are manual, ad-hoc test tools that allow you to quickly check the UI's underlying structure and properties. Investigation tools can also help you check the implementation of your logical hierarchy as well. UIA Verify, on the other hand, provides automated testing, where the framework has the ability to integrate into the test code and conduct regular, automated testing or spot checks of UIA test scenarios. The goal of the test framework is to promote consistent implementation across products and platforms (even those other than the Windows operating system). Because the source code is available for the framework, the code can be ported or enhanced for more advanced testing scenarios.

In addition to verifying the programmatic access, some of these tools can help you assess the implementation of your keyboard access, but, as you will learn, the tools can only go so far. So, it is important to manually verify that all of your scenarios can be accomplished with only the keyboard.

Although test tools can aid in confirming that your implementation meets the UIA Specification, ultimately, your end user's experience is what's vital to your product's success. Not only should the "nuts and bolts" of your application work and meet your users' needs as expected, but it should also be easy and intuitive for them to use, as well. In addition to obtaining feedback from a public beta release, observe users' overall experiences with your product through usability testing. You can also do heuristic evaluations internally by having employees within your company try your product and give you feedback. Because accessibility shares many requirements and best practices with many usability and UI design guidelines, you can focus on important user scenarios that impact many more users than you might have thought.

Accessibility Testing and Test Automation

While programmatic access to the UI is crucial for making software accessible today, the implementation for it is often reused by automated test tools and ATs in many different ways. Screen readers, for instance, announce desktop actions and keyboard input in speech recognition programs. On the other hand, automated test tools would use the accessibility API support for hit testing. Because of the diverse use of the accessibility API support, conflicts of interest can occur.

Before UIA, test automation used Microsoft Active Accessibility (MSAA), properties, such as accName, as unique and persistent identifiers to keep track of UI elements on-screen. The Name property was never intended to be used as a unique identifier among siblings, and using it as such can lead to unwanted results, polluting the accessibility object model by rendering a non-"human readable" string. The same rule applies to invisible or layout elements in the accessibility objects. The Name property should never be given a value of "MyAppHost," for instance, even if it is a layout object that is invisible to the users, or screen reader users may hear "MyAppHost" somewhere in your application. With UIA, a few new properties such as AutomationId, RuntimeId, and ClassName are introduced to help identify objects among siblings.

Go further: For UIA Properties and definitions go to http://go.microsoft.com/fwlink/?LinkId=150842.

Tools

For programmatic and keyboard requirements, there is no one tool that can verify your full implementation. Investigation tools and the UIA Verify framework are complementary. Investigation tools will allow you to manually check your implementation, while UIA Verify is automated and apply heuristics to help you verify that your implementation meets UIA Specification requirements. For keyboard access, manual testing should also be used to ensure access works for all navigation and user scenarios.

Depending on your control framework, there may be a variety of tools you may need to use for testing. The tools that we introduce are available on the Windows platform and can test UIA implementations. Regardless of the tools you use, remember that tools are only indicators your implementation may be wrong (or right). Try to use a variety of tools to verify your implementation and, when possible, find users of ATs, such as screen readers, to use your UI.

Investigation Tools

Investigation tools are manual test tools that allow you to quickly assess the UI for incorrect programmatic access implementations.

Inspect Objects (Inspect) and UI Spy are two investigation tools in the Microsoft Windows Software Development Kit (SDK) that provide a view of the programmatic implementation for the UI that uses a Windows Automation API, such as MSAA or UIA. They allow you to view the UI's underlying structure and properties, as well as interact with the elements, but they will only show you what was implemented and not indicate where your implementation is incorrect. As a result, you must understand the UI and all aspects of the accessibility framework that your product is built on, as well the output of results coming from the tool. Table 4-1 lists the pros and cons of these tools.

TABLE 4-1 Pros and cons of investigation tools

Pros	Cons
• Allows you to quickly investigate a UI. • Provides a raw view of the programmatic access in your product.	• You must understand the UI as well as output results from the tool. • Does not point out if there are problems with your implementation; you must rely on your knowledge to resolve any issues.

UI Spy also offers logging for UIA Events by types, as well as by scope. For instance, UI Spy can listen for StructureChanged UIA Events coming from a specific dialog box.

Accessible Event Watcher (AccEvent) is another investigation tool that will help you to assess your programmatic access. AccEvent is included in the MSAA SDK and allows you to review the WinEvents raised by the Windows Automation API.

Go further: For the Microsoft Windows SDK, go to http://go.microsoft.com/fwlink/?LinkId=150842.

UIA Verify Test Automation Framework

Intended to verify the implementation of the Windows Automation API, UIA Verify is a suite of test libraries that will help you test your UIA Provider implementations.

Using UIA Verify, you can write an automated test driver that runs a set of UIA test scenarios per the UIA Specification. You can also use the visual, front-end UI to run spot tests on built-in test scenarios. The tool will report the test results in XML or HTML format, and you can use that as a source for investigation requirements. Not all errors are obvious, and some errors suggest checking the validity of the problem. For example, because we rarely see a button control that can be accessible without a name, the test will report an error if your button control is left without a Name Property.

When UIA Verify alerts you to an error, use an investigation tool to look at the issue. Does the error seem reproducible? Visual UIA Verify, the front-end GUI of UIA Verify, can be handy to re-run the test with specific UI elements on screen. For some types of issues, you may need to use other investigation tools, such as Inspect or AccEvent, to keep track of object information at run time in greater details.

UIA Verify provides bugs about your accessible implementation, but their results are not conclusive. For instance, suppose you had a button visually labeled "OK." If you set its Name property to "Cancel," UIA Verify would only recognize that a button should have a programmatic name, but it would not be able to verify that the name is correct. In this case, UIA Verify would not raise an error. Final confirmation that the accessibility name matched the exact UI text on-screen would have to be done visually (optical character recognition technology may help to resolve such issues in the future, but it is still difficult to get to 100 percent accuracy as of today). Table 4-2 lists the pros and cons of UIA Verify.

TABLE 4-2 Pros and cons of the UIA Verify Test Automation Framework

Pros	Cons
• Can identify problems in your implementation.	• Cannot fully review your implementation.
• Provides recommendations on how to them.	• Errors indicated by UIA Verify are not conclusive.
• Can quickly give a rough idea on how well your implementation is working.	

Table 4-3 provides a summary and resource links for the investigation and verification test tools mentioned for testing the programmatic access and keyboard access of Win32 applications.

TABLE 4-3 Tools for Testing Programmatic and Keyboard Access

Tool	Description
Inspect Objects (Inspect)	Investigation tool that allows you to examine the element's patterns and properties as well as navigate the tree. Inspect allows you to interact with the elements through the accessibility APIs and navigate the elements by keyboard, mouse, or navigation methods provided by the framework.
Accessible Event Watcher (AccEvent)	Investigation tool that allows you to review events raised by the Windows Automation API. You can scope the events you want to listen to, the properties that should be included with those events, and which window to listen to for the events.
UI Spy	Investigation tool that allows you to examine the UIA Tree, Elements, and Events. UI Spy enables developers and testers to view and interact with the user interface (UI) elements of an application. By viewing the application's UI hierarchical structure, Property values, and raised Events, developers and testers can verify that the UI they are creating is programmatically accessible to assistive technology devices such as screen readers.
UI Automation Verify (UIA Verify) Test Automation Framework	Verification tool that checks your implementation at run time to confirm whether the UIA Provider is implementing correct tree, Patterns, and Properties. The UIA Verify facilitates manual and automated testing of the UIA Providers.

Go further: For more information and to download test tools, go to http://go.microsoft.com/fwlink/?LinkId=150842.

Keyboard

Because all applications must be navigable using only a keyboard, be sure to test your keyboard access. Try unplugging your mouse, and use only a keyboard to access all the functionality of your software. Ensure that the navigation via keyboard follows the order of controls that need keyboard focus.

Go further: For more information on testing keyboard accessibility and guidelines on designing keyboard access, go to http://go.microsoft.com/fwlink/?LinkId=150842.

Users and AT Devices

Throughout the development cycle, it is important to keep your users in mind. The earlier you can get feedback from actual users on your product, the less costly it is to incorporate their changes into your product. Although you may supplement your testing with third-party AT programs to test your work, beware that ATs can be complex, and you can very easily misinterpret the information you receive from them. So, it's a good idea to get users of AT to interact with your application by using the AT devices to (1) alert you to problems that your test tools might have missed and (2) to assess your users' experience with your product. If an issue does arise when using AT programs, try to isolate the scenario, and analyze the cause using the test tools mentioned in this chapter.

Delivery

Once your product has gone through testing, and necessary corrections have been made, it's time to deliver your product. Make sure that your implementation is properly documented and that the documentation is available in accessible formats. In your documentation, be sure to address the following questions:

- How did you address your users' needs? What did your programmatic access provide?

- How do you use your software with a keyboard? Do you expose a new UI that may be difficult to learn without the ability to see the screen? Your users may not use a mouse, so describing how to navigate a new UI by keyboard is very valuable information.

- What is the structure and implementation of your design? While end-users may not necessarily be interested in the technical details, AT vendors would find your specification very useful for optimizing the user experience.

- What did you not implement? Explain what was not implemented and what is not supported in your accessibility documentation. Document any workarounds if available.

Go further: For examples on declarations of conformance, go to http://go.microsoft.com/fwlink/?LinkId=150842.

Conclusion: 7 Steps to a Better Computing World

We now leave you with seven steps that we recommend for incorporating accessibility into your software development lifecycle:

1. Decide if accessibility is an important aspect to your software. If it is, learn and appreciate how it enables real users to live, work, and play, to help guide your design.

2. As you design solutions for your requirements, use controls provided by your framework (standard controls) as much as possible, and avoid any unnecessary effort and costs of custom controls.

3. Design a logical hierarchy for your product, noting where the standard controls, any custom controls, and keyboard focus are in the UI.

4. Design basic accessibility system settings (such as keyboard navigation, high contrast, and high dpi) into your product, according to your framework's accessibility requirements.

5. Implement your design, using the Microsoft Accessibility Developer Center and your framework's accessibility specification as a reference point.

6. Test your product to ensure that end users will be able to take advantage of the accessibility techniques implemented in it.

7. Deliver your finished product and document your accessible implementation.

It's very easy to get lost in the details of providing accessibility in your software, but with UIA, we believe that you can create flexible and intuitive products that support accessibility. With the number of accessible technology users expected to rise to 70 million by 2010, up from 57 million in 2003 (Forrester 2004), and with more than half of computer users today that could benefit from accessible technology (Forrester 2003), creating accessible products makes good business sense and is the right thing to do. Not only are you addressing the needs of those who need it, you are working to make the experience for all of your users better.

Go further: For more information on developing accessible products and to share ideas with other accessibility developers, go to http://go.microsoft.com/fwlink/?LinkId=150842.

References

Forrester Research, Inc. 2004. "Accessible Technology in Computing: Examining Awareness, Use, and Future Potential." Cambridge, MA. 41.

———. 2003. "The Wide Range of Abilities and Its Impact on Technology." Cambridge, MA. 10.

Appendix A
Windows Automation API: Overview

Source: "Windows Automation API SDK" from the Microsoft Developer Network (MSDN) Web site. To view this content online, go to *http://msdn.microsoft.com/en-us/library/ aa163327.aspx.*

Windows offers two application programming interface (API) specifications for user interface accessibility and software test automation: Microsoft Active Accessibility, and User Interface Automation (UI Automation). Microsoft Active Accessibility is the legacy API that was introduced in Windows 95 as a platform add-in. UI Automation is a Windows implementation of the User Interface Automation specification.

This section provides a high-level overview of Microsoft Windows Automation API 3.0, which includes the legacy Microsoft Active Accessibility API and the new UI Automation API. The overview highlights the similarities and differences between Microsoft Active Accessibility and UI Automation, describes the components and features that enable the two technologies to work together, and provides guidelines for choosing which technology to implement.

This section includes the following topics:

- Microsoft Active Accessibility and UI Automation Compared

- Architecture and Interoperability

- Limitations of Microsoft Active Accessibility

- UI Automation Specification

- The IAccessibleEX Interface

- Choosing Microsoft Active Accessibility, UI Automation, or IAccessibleEx

Microsoft Active Accessibility and UI Automation Compared

Although Microsoft Active Accessibility and Microsoft UI Automation are two different technologies, the basic design principles are similar. Both expose the UI object model as a hierarchical tree, rooted at the desktop. Microsoft Active Accessibility represents individual UI elements as *accessible objects*, and UI Automation represents them as *automation elements*. Both refer to the accessibility tool or software automation program as the *client*. However, Microsoft Active Accessibility refers to the application or control offering the UI for accessibility as the *server*, while UI Automation refers to this as the *provider*.

Microsoft Active Accessibility offers a single COM interface with a fixed, small set of properties. UI Automation offers a richer set of properties, as well as a set of extended interfaces called Control Patterns to manipulate accessible objects in ways Microsoft Active Accessibility cannot.

While UI Automation previously had both managed and unmanaged APIs for providers, the original release had no unmanaged interfaces for clients. Now, UI Automation clients can be written entirely in unmanaged code.

The latest framework also provides support for transitioning from Microsoft Active Accessibility servers to UI Automation providers. The IAccessibleEx interface specification enables support for specific UI Automation Patterns and Properties to be added to legacy Microsoft Active Accessibility servers without needing to rewrite the entire implementation. The specification also allows in-process Microsoft Active Accessibility clients to access UI Automation provider interfaces directly, rather than through UI Automation client interfaces.

The ecosystem of Windows automation technologies, called the Windows Automation API, includes classic Microsoft Active Accessibility and Windows implementations of the UI Automation specification. The UI Automation specification is implemented on many Microsoft products, including Windows 7, Windows Vista, Windows Server 2008, Windows Presentation Foundation (WPF), and Microsoft Silverlight.

Architecture and Interoperability

This section briefly describes the architecture of the Windows Automation technologies Microsoft Active Accessibility and Microsoft UI Automation, and the components that allow interoperability between applications based on the two different technologies.

Microsoft Active Accessibility Architecture

Microsoft Active Accessibility exposes basic information about custom controls such as control name, location on screen, and type of control, as well as state information such as visibility and enabled/disabled status. The UI is represented as a hierarchy of accessible objects; changes and actions are represented as WinEvents.

Microsoft Active Accessibility consists of the following components:

- **Accessible object**   A logical UI element (such as a button) that is represented by an IAccessible COM interface and an integer child identifier (ChildID).

- **WinEvents**   An event system that enables servers to notify clients when an accessible object changes.

- **OLEACC.dll**   The run-time, dynamic-link library that provides the Microsoft Active Accessibility API and the accessibility system framework. OLEACC implements proxy objects that provide default accessibility information for standard UI elements, including USER controls, USER menus, and common controls.

For Microsoft Active Accessibility, the system component of the accessibility framework (OLEACC) helps the communication between accessibility tools and applications, as the following illustration shows.

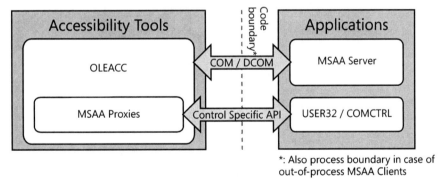

*: Also process boundary in case of out-of-process MSAA Clients

The applications (Microsoft Active Accessibility servers) provide UI accessibility information to tools (Microsoft Active Accessibility clients), which interact with the UI on behalf of users. The code boundary is both a programmatic and a process boundary.

UI Automation Architecture

With UI Automation, the UI Automation Core component (UIAutomationCore.dll) is loaded into both the accessibility tools' and applications' processes. The core component manages cross-process communication, provides higher level services such as searching for elements by Property values, and enables bulk fetching or caching of Properties, which provides better performance than the Microsoft Active Accessibility implementation.

UI Automation includes proxy objects that provide UI information about standard UI elements such as USER controls, USER menus, and common controls. It also includes proxies that enable UI Automation clients to get UI information from Microsoft Active Accessibility servers.

The following illustration shows the relationships among the various components in UI Automation providers (Accessibility Tools) and clients (Applications).

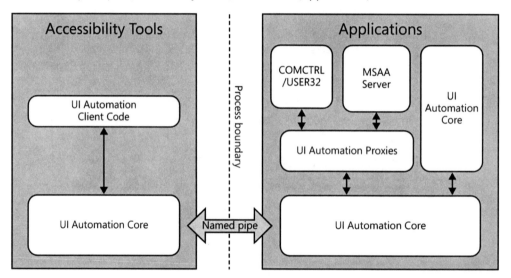

Interoperability Between Microsoft Active Accessibility-Based Applications and UI Automation-Based Applications

The UI Automation to Microsoft Active Accessibility Bridge enables Microsoft Active Accessibility clients to access UI Automation providers by converting the UI Automation object model to a Microsoft Active Accessibility object model. The following illustration shows the role of the UI Automation-to-Microsoft Active Accessibility Bridge.

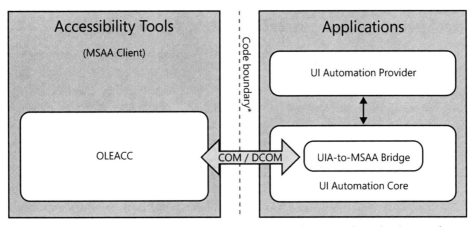

*: Also process boundary in case of
out-of-process MSAA Clients

Similarly, the Microsoft Active Accessibility-to-UI Automation Proxy translates Microsoft Active Accessibility-based server object models for UI Automation clients. The following illustration shows the role of the Microsoft Active Accessibility-to-UI Automation Proxy.

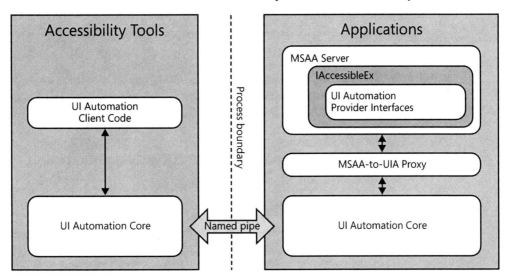

By using the IAccessibleEx interface, you can improve existing Microsoft Active Accessibility Server implementations by adding only required UI Automation object model information. The Microsoft Active Accessibility-to-UI Automation Proxy takes care of incorporating the added UI Automation object model. For more information, see the section of this appendix titled "The IAccessibleEx Interface."

Limitations of Microsoft Active Accessibility

Microsoft designed the Microsoft Active Accessibility object model about the same time as Windows 95 released. The model is based on "roles" defined a decade ago, and you cannot support new UI behaviors or merge two or more roles together. There is no text object model, for example, to help assistive technologies deal with complex Web content. UI Automation overcomes these limitations by introducing Control Patterns that enable objects to support more than one role, and the UI Automation Text Control Pattern offers a full-fledged text object model.

Another limitation involves navigating the object model. Microsoft Active Accessibility represents the UI as a hierarchy of accessible objects. Clients navigate from one accessible object to another using interfaces and methods available from the accessible object. Servers can expose the children of an accessible object with properties of the IAccessible interface, or with the standard IEnumVARIANT COM interface. Clients, however, must be able to deal with both approaches for any server. This ambiguity means extra work for client implementers, and broken accessible object models for server implementers.

UI Automation represents the UI as a hierarchical tree of Automation Elements, and provides a single interface for navigating the tree. Clients can customize the view of elements in the tree by scoping and filtering.

Finally, Microsoft Active Accessibility properties and functions cannot be extended without breaking or changing the IAccessible COM interface specification. The result is that new control behavior cannot be exposed through the object model; it tends to be static.

With UI Automation, as new UI elements are created, application developers can introduce custom Properties, Control Patterns, and Events to describe the new elements.

UI Automation Specification

The UI Automation specification provides flexible programmatic access to UI elements on the Windows desktop, enabling assistive technology products such as screen readers to provide information about the UI to end users and to manipulate the UI by means other than standard input. The specification can be supported across platforms other than Windows.

The implementation of UI Automation specification in Windows is also called UI Automation (UI Automation). UI Automation is broader in scope than just an interface definition. UI Automation provides:

- An object model and functions that make it easy for client applications to receive events, retrieve property values, and manipulate UI elements.

- A core infrastructure for finding and fetching across process boundaries.

- A set of interfaces for providers to express the tree structure, general properties, and functionality of UI elements.

- A "Control Type" property that allows clients and providers to clearly indicate the common properties, functionality, and structure of a UI object.

UI Automation improves on Microsoft Active Accessibility by:

- Enabling efficient out-of-process clients, while continuing to allow in-process access.

- Exposing more information about the UI in a way that allows clients to be out-of-process.

- Coexisting with and leveraging Microsoft Active Accessibility without inheriting its limitations. For more information, see the section of this appendix titled "Limitations of Microsoft Active Accessibility."

The implementation of the UI Automation specification in Windows features COM-based interfaces and managed interfaces.

UI Automation Elements

UI Automation exposes every piece of the UI to client applications as an *automation element*. Providers supply Property values for each element. Elements are exposed as a tree structure, with the desktop as the root element.

Automation Elements expose common properties of the UI elements they represent. One of these properties is the Control Type, which describes its basic appearance and functionality (for example, a button or a check box).

UI Automation Tree

The UI Automation tree represents the entire UI: the root element is the current desktop, and child elements are application windows. Each of these child elements can contain elements representing menus, buttons, toolbars, and so on. These elements in turn can contain elements like list items, as the following illustration shows.

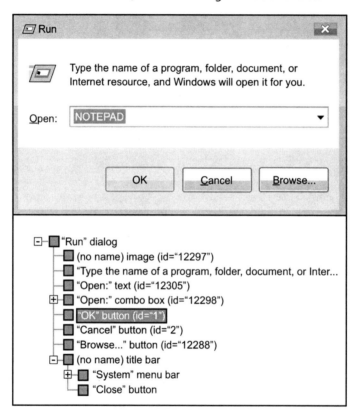

Be aware that the order of the siblings in the UI Automation tree is quite important. Objects that are next to each other visually should also be next to each other in the UI Automation tree.

UI Automation providers for a particular control support navigation among the child elements of that control. However, providers are not concerned with navigation between these control sub-trees. This is managed by the UI Automation core, using information from the default window providers.

To help clients process UI information more effectively, the framework supports alternative views of the automation tree: raw view, control view, and content view. As the following table shows, the type of filtering determines the views, and the client defines the scope of a view.

Automation Tree	Description
Raw view	The full tree of Automation Element objects for which the desktop is the root.
Control view	A subset of the raw view that closely maps to the UI structure as the user perceives it.
Content view	A subset of the control view that contains content most relevant to the user, like the values in a drop-down combo box.

UI Automation Properties

The UI Automation specification defines two kinds of properties: Automation Element Properties and Control Pattern Properties. Automation Element Properties apply to most controls, providing fundamental information about the element, such as its name. Control Pattern Properties apply to Control Patterns, which are described next.

Unlike with Microsoft Active Accessibility, every UI Automation Property is identified by a GUID and a programmatic name, which makes new Properties easier to introduce.

UI Automation Control Patterns

A Control Pattern describes a particular aspect of the functionality of an Automation Element. For example, a simple "click-able" control like a button or hyperlink should support the Invoke Control Pattern to represent the "click" action.

Each Control Pattern is a canonical representation of possible UI features and functions. The current implementation of UI Automation defines 22 Control Patterns. The Windows Automation API can also support custom Control Patterns. Unlike Microsoft Active Accessibility role or state properties, one Automation Element can support multiple UI Automation Control Patterns.

UI Automation Control Types

A Control Type is an Automation Element Property that specifies a well-known control that the element represents. Currently, UI Automation defines 38 Control Types, including Button, CheckBox, ComboBox, DataGrid, Document, Hyperlink, Image, ToolTip, Tree, and Window.

Before you can assign a Control Type to an element, the element needs to meet certain conditions, including a particular automation tree structure, Property values, Control Patterns, and Events. However, you are not limited to these. You can extend a control with custom Patterns and Properties, as well as with the pre-defined ones.

The total number of pre-defined Control Types is significantly lower than Microsoft Active Accessibility accRole definitions, because UI Automation Control Types can be combined to express a larger set of features while Microsoft Active Accessibility roles cannot.

UI Automation Events

UI Automation Events notify applications of changes to, and actions taken with Automation Elements. There are four different types of UI Automation Events, and they do not necessarily mean that the visual state of the UI has changed. The UI Automation Event model is independent of the WinEvent framework in Windows, although the Windows Automation API makes UI Automation Events interoperable with the Microsoft Active Accessibility framework.

The IAccessibleEx Interface

The IAccessibleEx interface enables existing applications or UI libraries to extend their Microsoft Active Accessibility object model to support UI Automation without rewriting the implementation from scratch. With IAccessibleEx, you can implement only the additional UI Automation Properties and Control Patterns needed to fully describe the UI and its functionality.

Because the Microsoft Active Accessibility-to-UI Automation Proxy translates the object models of IAccessibleEx-enabled Microsoft Active Accessibility servers as UI Automation object models, UI Automation clients do not need to do any extra work. The IAccessibleEx interface can also enable in-process Microsoft Active Accessibility clients to interact directly with UI Automation providers.

Choosing Microsoft Active Accessibility, UI Automation, or IAccessibleEx

If you are developing a new application or control, Microsoft recommends using UI Automation. Although Microsoft Active Accessibility can be easier to implement in the short term, the limitations inherent in this technology, such as its aging object model and inability to support new UI behaviors or merge rolls, makes it more difficult and costly over the long term. These limitations become especially apparent when introducing new controls. For more information, see the section of this appendix titled "Limitations of Microsoft Active Accessibility."

The UI Automation object model is easier to use and is more flexible than that of Microsoft Active Accessibility. The UI Automation Elements reflect the evolution of modern user interfaces, and developers can define custom UI Automation Control Patterns, Properties, and Events.

Microsoft Active Accessibility tends to run slowly for clients that run out of process. To improve performance, developers of accessibility tool programs often choose to hook into and run their programs in the target application process: an extremely difficult and risky approach. UI Automation is much easier to implement for out-of-process clients, and offers much better performance and reliability.

If you are updating an existing Microsoft Active Accessibility-based application or control, consider adding support for UI Automation by implementing the IAccessibleEx interface. First, ensure that your application or control meets the following requirements:

- The baseline Microsoft Active Accessibility server's hierarchy of accessible objects must be well-organized and error-free. IAccessibleEx cannot fix problems with existing accessible object hierarchies.

- Your IAccessibleEx implementation must comply with both the Microsoft Active Accessibility specification, and the UI Automation specification. Microsoft provides a set of tools for validating compliance with both specifications.

If either of these requirements is not met, consider implementing UI Automation natively. You can keep legacy Microsoft Active Accessibility server implementations for backward compatibility if it is necessary. From a UI Automation client's perspective, there is no difference between UI Automation providers and Microsoft Active Accessibility servers that implement IAccessibleEx correctly.

Appendix B
UI Automation Overview

Source: "Windows Automation API SDK" from the Microsoft Developer Network (MSDN) Web site. To view this content online, go to *http://msdn.microsoft.com/en-us/library/ aa163327.aspx*.

Microsoft UI Automation is an accessibility framework for Windows. It provides programmatic access to most user interface (UI) elements on the desktop. It enables assistive technology products, such as screen readers, to provide information about the UI to end users and to manipulate the UI by means other than standard input. UI Automation also allows automated test scripts to interact with the UI.

UI Automation was first available in Windows XP as part of the Microsoft .NET Framework. Although an unmanaged C++ API was also published at that time, the usefulness of client functions was limited because of interoperability issues. For Windows 7, the API has been rewritten in the Component Object Model (COM).

> **Note** Although the library functions introduced in the earlier version of UI Automation are still documented, they should not be used in new applications.

UI Automation client applications can be written with the assurance that they will work on multiple Windows control frameworks. The UI Automation core masks any differences in the frameworks that underlie various pieces of the UI. For example, the Content property of a Windows Presentation Foundation (WPF) button, the Caption property of a Win32 button, and the ALT property of an HTML image are all mapped to a single Property, Name, in the UI Automation view.

UI Automation provides full functionality in Windows XP, Windows Server 2003, and later operating systems.

UI Automation providers are components that implement UI Automation support on controls and offer some support for Microsoft Active Accessibility client applications, through a built-in bridging service.

> **Note** UI Automation does not enable communication between processes that are started by different users through the **Run as** command.

This appendix contains the following sections:

- UI Automation Components

- UI Automation Header Files

- UI Automation Model

- UI Automation Providers

UI Automation Components

UI Automation has four main components, as shown in the following table.

Component	Description
Provider API	A set of COM interfaces that are implemented by UI Automation providers. UI Automation providers are objects that provide information about UI elements and respond to programmatic input.
Client API	A set of COM interfaces that enable client applications to obtain information about the UI and to send input to controls. **Note** The functions described in Deprecated Control Pattern Functions and Deprecated Node Functions are obsolete and in the process of being removed. Instead, client applications should use the UI Automation COM interfaces described in UI Automation Element Interfaces for Clients.
UiAutomationCore.dll	The run-time library, sometimes called the UI Automation core, that handles communication between providers and clients.
OLEACC.dll	The run-time library for Microsoft Active Accessibility and the proxy objects. The library also provides proxy objects used by the MSAA-to-UIA Proxy to support Win32 controls.

There are two ways of using UI Automation: to create support for custom controls by using the provider API, and to create client applications that use the UI Automation core to communicate with UI elements. Depending on your focus, you should refer to different parts of the documentation.

UI Automation Header Files

The UI Automation API is defined in several different C/C++ header files that are included with the Microsoft Windows Software Development Kit (SDK). The UI Automation header files are described in the following table.

Header file	Description
uiautomationclient.h	Defines the interfaces and related programming elements used by UI Automation clients.
uiautomationcore.h	Defines the interfaces and related programming elements used by UI Automation providers.
uiautomationcoreapi.h	Defines general constants, GUIDs, data types, and structures used by UI Automation clients and providers. It also contains definitions for the deprecated node and Control Pattern functions.
uiautomation.h	Includes all of the other UI Automation header files. Because most UI Automation applications require elements from all UI Automation header files, it is best to include uiautomation.h in your UI Automation application projects instead of including each file individually.

If you are developing an application that uses the UI Automation API, you should include uiautomation.h in your project. If your application supports Microsoft Active Accessibility, include the oleacc.h header file. UI Automation applications that use GUIDs also require the initguid.h header file. If needed, initguid.h should be included before uiautomation.h.

UI Automation Model

UI Automation exposes every element of the UI to client applications as an object represented by the IUIAutomationElement interface. Elements are contained in a tree structure, with the desktop as the root element. Clients can filter the raw view of the tree as a control view or a content view. These standard views of the structure can easily be seen by using the UI Spy application that is included with the Windows SDK. Applications can also create custom views.

A UI Automation Element exposes properties of the control or UI element that it represents. One of these properties is the Control Type, which defines the basic appearance and functionality of the control or UI element as a single recognizable entity, for example, a button or check box.

In addition, a UI Automation Element exposes one or more Control Patterns. A Control Pattern provides a set of Properties that are specific to a particular Control Type. A Control Pattern also exposes methods that enable client applications to get more information about the element and to provide input to the element.

Note There is no one-to-one correspondence between Control Types and Control Patterns. A Control Pattern may be supported by multiple Control Types, and a control may support multiple Control Patterns, each of which exposes different aspects of its behavior. For example, a combo box has at least two Control Patterns: one that represents its ability to expand and collapse, and another that represents the selection mechanism. However, a control can exhibit only a single Control Type.

UI Automation provides information to client applications through events. Unlike WinEvents, UI Automation Events are not based on a broadcast mechanism. UI Automation clients register for specific Event notifications and can request that specific Properties and Control Pattern information be passed to their event handlers. In addition, a UI Automation Event contains a reference to the element that raised it. Providers can improve performance by raising Events selectively, depending on whether any clients are listening.

Go further: Go to http://go.microsoft.com/fwlink/?LinkId=150842 for more information on the following topics:

- Deprecated Control Pattern Functions

- Deprecated Node Functions

- UI Automation Element Interfaces for Clients

- UI Automation Control Types Overview

- UI Automation Control Patterns Overview

- UI Automation Events Overview

UI Automation Providers

After designing your implementation, you must implement a provider interface to support your implementation. For more details on how to do so, go to *http://go.microsoft.com/fwlink/?LinkId=150842.*

Glossary

Accessibility The quality of a system incorporating hardware or software that makes it usable by people with one or more physical disabilities, such as restricted mobility, blindness, or deafness.

Accessibility Interoperability Alliance (AIA) A group of information technology (IT) and assistive technology (AT) companies, content providers, and other engineering organizations that collaborate together to create standards and design solutions for interoperable accessible technology.

Accessible Event Watcher (AccEvent) An investigation tool that allows you to review events raised by the Windows Automation API.

Alternative Text (Alt Text) A short descriptive summary of the content shown in a figure. The text provides an alternative means of understanding what the art depicts if a user cannot see the art. It is particularly useful for users who are visually impaired (whether or not they use screen readers to interpret the text in a document) and those who prefer to turn off images, such as users who have slow Internet connections, use a text-only browser, or prefer to work more rapidly than image downloading allows.

Application Programming Interface (API) A set of routines, data structures, object classes, or protocols provided by libraries or operating system services in order to support the building of applications.

Assistive Technology (AT) A specialty product designed to provide additional accessibility to individuals who have physical or cognitive difficulties, impairments, and disabilities.

Automation Element An element in UI Automation that exposes common properties of the UI element it represents.

Automation ID An Automation Element Property used to identify an element. This Property should be filled out for most elements.

Beta A new software or hardware product, or one that is being updated, that is released to users for the purpose of evaluation in the real world.

Bug An error in coding or logic that causes a program to malfunction or to produce incorrect results. Minor bugs, such as a cursor that does not behave as expected, can be inconvenient or frustrating, but do not damage information. More severe bugs can require the user to restart the program or the computer, losing whatever previous work had not been saved.

Child In a tree structure, the relationship of a node to its immediate predecessor. Also see parent/child. In contrast to sibling.

Client An accessibility or test automation tool that uses an accessibility API to programmatically access application user interfaces.

Common Controls A set of windows that are implemented by the common control library, which is a dynamic-link library (DLL) included with the Windows operating system.

Control A component in an application with a visual representation in the UI that can be manipulated by the user to perform an action.

Control Pattern In UI Automation, a control attribute or functionality that represents common UI behaviors (such as invoking a button) and supports the UIA Properties, Methods, and Events.

Control Type A pre-defined set of patterns, properties, and conditions used to define a **control**'s basic appearance and functionality. A well-known identifier that indicates the kind of control a particular UI element represents, such as a combo box or a button.

Custom Control A **control** that is not provided by the **UI** framework; or a modified control based on a standard control.

Depth-First Search Generally following a top-to-bottom, left-to-right scheme, a tree traversal pattern that starts at the root of a tree (located at the top of the tree) and moves down any branches of each top-level node before traversing the next top-level node.

Digital Inclusion The idea of using technology to its fullest potential by looking for opportunities to innovate and improve the user experience for all users, including improving issues of accessibility.

Disability A temporary or permanent impairment that may involve visual, hearing, mobility, cognitive, or speech abilities.

Element In a logical hierarchy, a node representing a control in the UI.

Event An action or occurrence, often generated by the user, to which a program might respond (for example, key presses, button clicks, or mouse movements). In UI Automation, Events are action notifications that correspond to an activity occurring in the UI.

Framework In object-oriented programming, a reusable basic design structure, consisting of abstract and concrete classes, which assists in building applications.

High Contrast A system setting that heightens the color contrast of some text and images on your computer screen, making those items more distinct and easier to identify. Increasing the contrast in colors reduces eyestrain and makes things easier to read for many people.

High Dots Per Inch (High DPI) Dots per inch is a measure of screen and printer resolution that is expressed as the number of dots that a device can print or display per linear inch. Resolutions of 144 dpi or higher are considered high dpi. Since the release of Windows Vista, the Windows platform replaced large font settings with dpi configurations.

IAccessible A COM-based interface in MSAA that exposes information about UI elements. IAccessible is always paired with ChildId to make up one UI element representation (called "Accessible Object" in MSAA).

Implementation Table A table that lists the control types, patterns, and properties for implementing accessible controls.

In-Process In the context of accessibility APIs, in-process refers to a program that is running within the process of a target application. For instance, some programs use in-process hooks and load a part of their code to target applications.

Inspect Objects (Inspect) A Windows Automation API investigation tool that allows you to examine the element's Patterns and Properties as well as navigate the tree. Inspect allows you to interact with the elements through the accessibility APIs and navigate the elements by keyboard, mouse, or navigation methods provided by the framework.

Investigation Tools Investigation tools are manual test tools that allow you to quickly assess the **UI** for issues. Allows you to look at your UI's underlying structure and properties, as well as interact with the elements. Investigation tools do not "problem-solve" for you.

Information Technology Industry Council (ITIC) A lobbying organization based in Washington, D.C., that assists member high-tech companies to achieve legislative policy objectives.

Library In programming, a collection of routines stored in a file. Each set of instructions in a library has a name, and each performs a different task.

Logical Hierarchy A systematic mapping of the controls in an application to programmatically exposed elements in UIA. The logical hierarchy provides context for the controls' location and relationships in the UI and helps to determine the controls'

implementation. It can also be used for planning keyboard navigation and other system settings.

Microsoft Accessibility Developer Center A portal for guidance, essential information, and tools and technologies for developing accessible applications and writing accessible code for Microsoft developers.

Microsoft Developer Network (MSDN) A portal for developers using Microsoft products, which allows developers to learn, share information, and download tools.

Microsoft UI Automation Community Promise A specification that provides information about Microsoft's accessibility frameworks, including Active Accessibility, UI Automation, and its shared implementations. Intended for interoperable implementations by other companies. Access the UI Automation Specification from the Microsoft Accessibility Developer Center at *http://msdn.microsoft.com/en-us/accessibility/default.aspx*.

Microsoft Active Accessibility (MSAA) A COM-based accessibility **API**, first released in 1997 as an add-on for Windows 95.

Node In tree structures, a location on the tree that can have links to one or more nodes below it. Some authors make a distinction between node and element, with an element being a given data type and a node comprising one or more elements as well as any supporting data structures.

Oleacc.dll A Windows operating system component that provides the platform support for MSAA.

On-Screen Keyboard An assistive technology that allows users to type and interact with their computer using an alternative input device like a switch, rather than the physical keyboard. An on-screen keyboard displays a visual keyboard with all of the standard keys.

Out-of-Process In the context of accessibility APIs, out-of-process refers to a program or script running outside of the target application processes.

Parent/child Pertaining to or constituting a relationship between nodes in a tree data structure in which the parent is one step closer to the root (that is, one level higher) than the child. In contrast to sibling.

Persona A fictional person who represents a major user group, based on real user data.

Platform In everyday usage, the type of computer or operating system being used. In this book, platform is only used when referring to the Windows platform.

Product Lifecycle The process by which a product is designed, developed, and released to market. The product lifecycle consists of three phases: (1) product definition, (2) product development, and (3) product servicing. Within these phases are the iterative stages of establishing requirements, design, implementation, verification, and release.

Programmatic Access Achieved when an application or library of UI functionality exposes the content, interactions, context, and semantics of the UI via a discoverable and publicly-documented application programming interface (API). The API can be used by another program to provide an augmentative, automated, or alternate, user interaction. Basic information conveyed through programmatic access includes: navigation, interactive elements, asynchronous changes to the page, keyboard focus, and other important information about the UI.

Property A characteristic or parameter expressed as a value used to describe a UI element. In UIA, Properties enable client applications to retrieve information about controls.

Provider In the context of UI Automation, providers expose information about the UI. Providers can be a full scale application or UI framework that supplies accessible UI parts to programs for agile software development. Providers are referred to as "servers" in MSAA because its role appears as a component object model (COM) server of the IAccessible interface paired with the ChildId.

Rasterization The conversion of vector graphics (images described in terms of mathematical elements, such as points and lines) to equivalent images composed of pixel patterns that can be stored and manipulated as sets of bits.

Screen Magnifier Also called a "screen enlarger," an assistive technology that works like a magnifying glass for the computer by enlarging a portion of the screen, which can increase legibility and make it easier to see items on the computer. Some screen magnifiers allow a person to zoom in and out on a particular area of the screen.

Screen Reader A software program that presents graphics and text as speech. A screen reader is used to verbalize, or "speak," everything on the screen include ing names and descriptions of control buttons, menus, text, and punctuation.

Section 508 of the Rehabilitation Act of 1996 An act for U.S. federal agencies procuring electronic and information technology. For further details, see *http://www.section508.gov/*.

Sibling A process or node in a data tree that is descended from the same immediate ancestor(s) as other processes or nodes. The order of sibling relationships is important when designing navigation. In contrast to **parent/child**.

Specification (spec) An explicit set of requirements to be satisfied by a material, product, or service.

System-Wide Settings Settings, such as font, screen resolution, or color settings, that allow users to customize the UI to fit their needs and preferences. System-wide settings should be respected and should work with your product.

Tab Order The specified sequential order by which users navigate through the **UI** using the TAB key or SHIFT+TAB.

Tab Stop The location, usually on an element that receives keyboard focus, where the cursor stops when the TAB key is pressed.

UI Automation (UIA) The new accessibility and automation framework for Windows. UIA provides programmatic access to user interface (UI) elements on the desktop, enabling assistive technology (AT) products such as screen readers to provide information about the UI to end users.

UI Automation (UIA) Tree A UIA-specific solution that helps assistive technologies gather information about the UI and its elements. The root element of the UIA Tree is the desktop, whose child elements are programs running on it, such as an application or the operating system's UI. The UIA Tree is not a fixed structure and is seldom seen in its totality, because it might contain thousands of elements. Parts of it are built as they are needed, and it can undergo changes as elements are added, moved, or removed. The UIA Tree should not be confused with the logical hierarchy, another treelike structure used for design purposes.

UI Spy An investigation tool that allows you to examine the UIA Tree, Elements, and Events. UI Spy enables developers and testers to view and interact with the user interface (UI) elements of an application. By viewing the application's UI hierarchical structure, Property values, and raised Events, developers and testers can verify that the UI they are creating is programmatically accessible to assistive technology devices such as screen readers.

UI Automation Verify (UIA Verify) Test Automation Framework A verification tool that checks your implementation at run time to confirm that you are implementing the correct tree, Patterns, and Properties. The framework facilitates manual and automated testing of the Microsoft UIA Provider implementation of a control or application.

Usability The extent to which a product can be used by specified users to achieve specified goals with effectiveness, efficiency and satisfaction in a specified context of use (ISO 9241-11). In general, how well users can learn and use a product to achieve their goals and how satisfied they are with that process.

User Experience (UX) The end-user's overall experience and satisfaction interacting with a product or service. In UI design, UX can touch on many fields of study, such as **usability**, human-computer interaction, and behavioral psychology.

User Interface (UI) The means by which humans can interact with a computer, technical device, or some other complex tool to accomplish a task.

User Scenario A test scenario in which a feature of the program is highly visible or necessary to successfully use your program. The feature tested is used by a majority of the application's users.

Voluntary Product Accessibility Template (VPAT) A standardized form developed by the Information Technology Industry Council (ITI) used to show how a software product meets key regulations of Section 508 of the Rehabilitation Act. VPATs were created as a collaborative effort between industry and ITI, and the U.S. government's General Services Administration (GSA) to evaluate and describe the accessibility of a product.

Windows Automation API The ecosystem of Windows automation technologies, which includes classic Microsoft Active Accessibility (MSAA) and Windows implementations of the UI Automation (UIA) specification.

Windows Presentation Foundation (WPF) A framework for programming that keeps the business code and the design layers separate. It uses Microsoft's newest accessibility API, UI Automation (UIA), to programmatically expose information to users of assistive technology (AT). Developers use the WPF code as well as its declarative markup language XAML to create products with amazing capabilities.

WinEvents A cross-process event system in the Windows platform that allows programs to notify others with a defined set of IDs and the information.

Workaround A way of bypassing a problem or functionality issue in a program.

Go further: The terms used in this book are based on definitions from the UI Automation (UIA) Specification, Windows Accessibility Software Developer Kit (SDK), the Microsoft Developer Network (MSDN), and the Microsoft Press Computer Dictionary. To access or learn more about these sources, go to http://go.microsoft.com/fwlink/?LinkId=150842.

Index

A

accessibility
  defined, 69
  incorporating into development lifecycle, 51
Accessibility Interoperability Alliance (AIA), 69
Accessible Event Watcher, 48–49, 69
alternative text for graphics, 11, 69
APIs, 69. *See also* Microsoft Active Accessibility API; UI Automation API
application programming interfaces (APIs), 69. *See also* Microsoft Active Accessibility API; UI Automation API
applications. *See* providers
arrow keys, navigating with, 24
assistive technology (AT) products. *See* ATs (assistive technology products)
ATs (assistive technology products). *See also* clients
  defined, 69
  order in which elements read, 13
  overview of, 1
  standard mapping scheme, 14
  user feedback on, 50
automated test drivers, 48
Automation Elements
  Control Types and Patterns, 3
  defined, 69
  overview of, 59
  properties, 6, 32–34, 61
  structure of, 3
Automation Events, 62
Automation IDs, 69
automation tree. *See* UIA Tree

B

beta products, 69
bugs, 69
button control, 3

C

calendar grid control, 33–34
child elements, 69
clients
  actions performed by, 2–3
  defined, 69
  provider communication with, 1–2
ComboBox control, 3
Common Controls, 69
containers
  defined, 12
  in logical hierarchies, 12
content view of UIA Tree, 5, 61
contextual elements, vs. decorative, 24
control libraries, 15
Control Patterns
  correlation to Control Types, 68
  custom, 7
  for custom controls, determining which apply, 31–32, 36–37
  defined, 29, 70
  examples of, 3, 5
  overview of, 5, 61
  properties. *See* properties
  Properties, required, 35–36
  supported in UI Automation, 15
  in Windows Automation API, 61
Control Types
  assigning to elements, 61
  Automation Element Properties, 32–34
  correlation to Control Patterns, 68
  defined, 29, 70
  examples of, 3
  generic, 6
  mapping, 16
  mapping custom controls to, 27, 31–38
  multiple elements for, marking, 21

overview of, 5, 61
  pre-defined, number of, 62
  supported in UI Automation, 15
control view of UIA Tree, 4, 61
controls. *See also* custom controls
  Control Patterns and Properties, determining, 36
  defined, 70
  designing, 9
  determining which need custom UIA solutions, 28
  functionality, determining, 36–37
  generic control type for, 6
  mapping, 11, 22
  programmatic access to, 43
  standard, advantages of, 25
  standard, identifying, 20
  standard, UI framework guidelines and, 27
  structures, examining, 22
custom controls
  Control Patterns, determining which apply, 31–32
  defined, 70
  identifying, 16, 20
  implementation table for, 30
  mapping to UIA Control Type, 27, 31–38, 40
  native UIA solutions. *See* native UIA solutions for controls
  publishing Control Type specifications, 41
  UIA Methods, determining required, 42
  UIA Specification list, checking against, 37–38

D

data grids, 12. *See also* containers
DataGrid Control Type, 32–33
decorative elements, vs. contextual, 24

product lifecycle
  accessibility considerations
    for, 51
  defined, 72
programmatic access
  defined, 72
  testing, 45
programmatically significant
  elements, defined, 16
properties, 61
  changes in, event for, 7
  for Control Patterns, 35–36
  custom, 7
  for custom controls, 32–34
  for custom controls,
    determining which apply,
    36–37
  defined, 29, 72
  specifications for, 6
  in UI Automation
    specification, 61
prototypes, 15
providers
  actions performed by, 2
  communication with clients,
    1–2
  defined, 72
  overview of, 1

R

rasterization, 72
raw view of UIA Tree, 4, 61
relationships, element, 12
  in logical hierarchies, 22–23

S

screen magnifiers, 72
screen readers. *See also* ATs
    (assistive technology
    products); clients
  defined, 73
  order of elements read by, 13
Selection Pattern property, 35
specifications, 73
standard controls
  advantages of, 25
  UI framework guidelines and,
    27
structuring UI. *See* logical
    hierarchy
system-wide settings, 73

T

tab order, 73
tab stops, 73
table format for logical
    hierarchy, 14
Table Pattern property, 35
testing
  automated drivers for, 48
  conflicts of interest when, 46
  with investigation tools. *See*
    investigation tools
  keyboard access, 45, 49
  programmatic access, 45
  tools for, using variety of, 47
  with UIA Verify. *See* UIA Verify
timecard example of logical
    hierarchy, 18–19
tree structure. *See* UIA Tree

U

UI accessibility APIs. *See* UI
    Automation API
UI Automation. *See* UIA (UI
    Automation)
UI Automation API, 66
  architecture of, 56
  benefits of, 59
  interoperability with Microsoft
    Active Accessibility API,
    56–57
  vs. Microsoft Active
    Accessibility API, 54
  properties in, 61
  proxy objects in, 56
  recommended, 62–63
  specification for, 58–59
  UI element representation
    in, 54
  unmanaged code, 54
  updating Microsoft Active
    Accessibility with, 63
UI Automation core, 66
UI Automation Elements. *See*
    Automation Elements
UI Automation Events, 62
UI design, 9–10
  intuitive, 25
  navigational order, 12–13,
    16, 19
UI elements
  binding other objects. *See*
    containers

control types for. *See* Control
    Types
decorative vs. contextual, 24
defined, 70
diagramming. *See* logical
    hierarchy
functionality, designing, 25
grouping. *See* containers
identifying for logical
    hierarchy, 16
keyboard focus, 43
MSAA properties as
    identifiers, 46
multiple, for Control Type, 21
naming, 11
navigational order, 19
order in which read by ATs, 13
overview of, 11
programmatically significant,
    16
properties. *See* properties
relationships, in logical
    hierarchy, 12, 22–23
UI framework
  choosing, 9
  decisions dependent on, 43
  defined, 70
UI hierarchy. *See* logical
    hierarchy
UI implementation table, 30, 70
UI prototypes, 15
UI Spy, 47, 49, 67, 73
UI testing. *See* testing
UIA (UI Automation)
  applications in. *See* providers
  ATs and, 1. *See also* ATs
    (assistive technology
    products)
  components of, 66
  Control Types supported in,
    15
  defined, 73
  events. *See* UIA Events
  goals of, 1
  header files, 66–67
  history of, 65
  interface for, 67–68
  model for, 67–68
  native solutions for controls.
    See native UIA solutions for
    controls
  navigation through UI. *See*
    UIA Tree

What do you think of this book?

We want to hear from you!

To participate in a brief online survey, please visit:

microsoft.com/learning/booksurvey

...and enter this book's ISBN number (appears above barcode on back cover).

Tell us how well this book meets your needs—what works effectively, and what we can do better. Your feedback will help us continually improve our books and learning resources for you.

Thank you in advance for your input!

Where to find the ISBN on back cover

Example only. Each book has unique ISBN.

Stay in touch!

To subscribe to the *Microsoft Press® Book Connection Newsletter*—for news on upcoming books, events, and special offers—please visit:

microsoft.com/learning/books/newsletter

LaVergne, TN USA
04 February 2011
215383LV00003B/87-110/P